SIGNS

OF THE

TIMES

**What the Bible says about
the Rapture, Antichrist,
Armageddon, Heaven, Hell,
and Other Issues of Our Day**

SIGNS OF THE TIMES

Unless otherwise indicated, all Scripture quotations are taken from: *The Holy Bible*, New King James Version © 1984 by Thomas Nelson, Inc.

Scripture quotations marked (NIV) are from *The Holy Bible*, New International Version®, NIV®. Copyright © 1973, 1978, 1984 by International Bible Society. Used by permission of Zondervan Publishing House.

Scripture quotations marked (TLB) are taken from *The Living Bible*, copyright © 1971 by Tyndale House Publishers, Wheaton, Illinois.

Scripture quotations marked (NLT) are taken from The New Living Translation, copyright © 1996, 2004 by Tyndale Charitable Trust. Used by permission of Tyndale House Publishers. All rights reserved.

Scripture quotations marked (THE MESSAGE) are taken from *The Message*, by Eugene Peterson. Copyright © 1993, 1994, 1995, 1996, 2000, 2001, 2002. Used by permission of NavPress Publishing Group. All rights reserved.

Scripture quotations marked (PHILLIPS) are from *The New Testament in Modern English*, Revised Edition © 1958, 1960, 1972 by J. B. Phillips.

ISBN: 978-0-9834004-3-1

Published by: Kerygma Publishing—Allen David Books, Dana Point, California
Coordination: FM Management, Ltd., Dana Point, California
www.kerygmapublishing.com
Contact: fmmgt@cox.net
34332 Port Lantern
Dana Point, CA 92629

Cover design: Ty Mattson
Interior design & Production: Highgate Cross+Cathey

Printed in the United States of America

CONTENTS

Chapter One

CONVERGING SIGNS

Don't be naive. There are difficult times ahead.
—2 Timothy 3:1, The Message

I heard a story about some Christians who were standing by the side of the road holding up a sign. Their hand-lettered placard read, "The end is near. Turn yourself around now before it's too late!"

Seeing their sign, a driver slammed on his brakes, rolled down his window and yelled, "You stupid Christians! Why don't you just leave people alone?" With that, he rolled up the window, gunned his engine, and sped down the road.

In another moment, there was a big splash.

One of the Christians turned to the other and said, "Do you think we should just put up a sign that says, 'Bridge Out' instead?"

Is the end of the world really near, or is this just another verse of the same old song about "the end times"? Haven't we heard all this before? In the children's story, Chicken Little got everyone in the barnyard all ramped up about the sky falling. But it never fell. Then there was that boy who kept crying, "Wolf! Wolf!" But the wolf never came, and eventually people got tired of hearing it, and stopped paying attention.

Most of us who have been believers for a number of years have heard talk about "the last days" again and again—all this business about our being the last generation before the return of Jesus Christ to this earth.

The truth is, nearly every generation in recent history has interpreted Bible prophecy in light of its own historical experience and the headlines of the day. Generation after generation has felt convinced they would be the last, and obviously…they weren't. They were wrong. So why should our generation be any different?

It's a legitimate question. And here is my answer. The Bible gives us certain signs of the times we're told to be looking for—clear indications that will alert us to Christ's soon return. And here's what I find so fascinating: There are more of those signs in closer proximity to one another than I have ever seen before.

If those warning signals mean anything—and I believe they do—we may be very, very close to the return of Jesus Christ.

I'm reminded of the little boy who was over at his grandmother's house, and loved to sit in the front room and listen to the big grandfather clock chime on the hour. His favorite time was lunch, because that's when it would chime twelve times in a row.

One day as lunchtime rolled around, the boy ran to the grandfather clock to listen to it toll. *Bong…bong…bong….* It chimed 8, 9, 10, 11, 12…*13, 14, 15, 16 times!* As it turned out, there was something wrong with the mechanism of the clock, and it went on chiming after the prescribed number.

Stunned, the boy ran to his grandmother who was making lunch in the kitchen. "Grandma! Grandma!" he yelled. "It's later than it has ever been before!"

That's true for our world as well. We are—quite literally—nearer to the world's final days than we have ever been before. People in the nineteenth and twentieth centuries who were alert to the biblical signs were right in saying that the time was drawing near—and now we're just that much nearer.

Escalating Signs

Here is one indicator of the Lord's return you may not have considered. One of the clear signs that we are in the end times is that people keep saying there's no way we could be in the end times!

Not long ago, I did a radio interview where the host had me on the air with some college professor who wanted to challenge my belief that Christ was coming back.

"Well sir," I said to the professor at one point, "I believe that you—yourself—are actually a fulfillment of Bible prophesy."

I don't think he'd ever heard anything like that before. "Why would you say that?" he demanded. "Why would you think I am a fulfillment of prophesy?"

In answer, I opened my Bible to 2 Peter 3, and read:

> First, I want to remind you that in the last days there will be scoffers who will laugh at the truth and do every evil thing they desire. This will be their argument: 'Jesus promised to come back, did he? Then where is he? Why, as far back as anyone can remember, everything has remained exactly the same since the world was first created'. (vv. 3-4, NLT)

Yes, in a sense "we've heard it all before," and time has marched on. But for those of us who are paying attention, the evidence keeps mounting—and even escalating in intensity and frequency.

For instance…. We continue to witness the *rapid escalation of global wars and terrorism*. Our world has experienced terrorism for many years, but never on the scale that we've seen since September 11, 2001. And now, as I write these words over ten years after that event, we see open conflict breaking out across the Middle East—even in nations once thought to be "stable." Revolutions have hit these nations like dominoes…Iran, Tunisia, Egypt, Libya, Syria, Bahrain, Saudi Arabia, Bahrain, and Yemen. The unrest in these Moslem nations is palpable. Where will it end?

We see the unprecedented increase in massive, *killer earthquakes* —absolutely stunning in their severity. Within recent months Haiti, Chile, and New Zealand have been shaken, with great property damage and loss of life. A recent quake in Japan was recorded at a shocking 9.0 on the Richter Scale, virtually devastating parts of that island nation. The earthquake was so violent that scientists believe the axis of the earth actually changed, and the entire island of Japan moved ten feet. Following that, of course, was a tsunami so vast and terrible it made Hollywood disaster epics look tame by comparison. When those waves slammed into some of the nation's nuclear power plants, it launched yet another major disaster, precipitating nuclear meltdowns and the release of deadly radioactivity.

Every day that goes by, the headlines speak of a *push for "globalization,"* "world unity," "one-world government," and a "world currency." You can hear almost constant chatter now about a "cashless society."

Another unmistakable sign of the end is the false teaching that has permeated the church. Yes, Christianity has endured *false teaching* since its earliest days. Speaking personally, however, in my thirty-plus years of ministry I have never seen such teaching making inroads as it has in the last few years. This too is a "sign of the times"—and might even be called a great apostasy.

Any one or two of these indicators would be significant enough. But it is the convergence of these events—so many signs at one time—that has me wondering if this will truly be the generation that will witness the return of Jesus Christ for His church.

Why do I say this? Because the Bible says this.

When speaking of the signposts that will mark the end of this age, the Bible tells us to look for an increase in the frequency of such events. The idea conveyed is that of a woman about to go into labor. As the time for the birth draws near, the pains come closer together—and grow more intense.

In 1 Thessalonians 5, Paul writes:

> For you know quite well that the day of the Lord will come unexpectedly, like a thief in the night. When people are saying, 'All is well; everything is peaceful and secure,' then disaster will fall upon them as suddenly as a woman's birth pains begin when her child is about to be born. And there will be no escape. (vv. 2-3, NLT)

Close and Closer

So when we look at the prophetic signs, they point to a period of time that will begin with the emergence of the Antichrist, and end with the return of Jesus Christ as King of kings and Lord of lords. The appearance of the Antichrist inaugurates a seven-year period known as the Great Tribulation. After the Antichrist shows his true colors, erects an image of himself in the rebuilt temple in Jerusalem, and commands people to worship it (an event known as the "abomination of desolation"), the world will enter a time when no one can buy or sell without the mark of the beast. Concurrent with this event, a savage persecution will be unleashed against Jews and against Christians—believers in the one true God.

Could the Antichrist be on the scene somewhere right now, just waiting to step out on the world's stage? Yes, I believe he could. And as far as we know, he might be on the world's stage already—just out of the spotlight. We could be very close to the emergence of this great enemy who will do the bidding of his master, Satan.

But here's the good news.

If Antichrist is close, Jesus Christ is even closer.

It is my firm belief that the Antichrist can't even be revealed until Christ comes for His people in the rapture of the church. So as close as we may be to the climax of history and the death agonies of this current world, we are that much closer to the moment when Jesus Christ will call His sons and daughters to Himself, and meet us in the air.

Yes, I know that good people differ on this topic. I have friends in ministry today who don't hold this view of the timing of the rapture. I think they're wrong, but I still love them. I would never break fellowship with someone over a different view on the order of end-time events.

But on this we must agree. *Jesus Christ is coming back again.* This is a fact clearly taught in Scripture, and no Bible-believing Christian would ever dispute that truth.

After the Lord's ascension to heaven, when the disciples were all standing around with their necks craned toward the sky where their Lord had just disappeared, two angels appeared and their side, and said: "Men of Galilee…why do you stand here looking into the sky? This same Jesus, who has been taken from you into heaven, will come back in the same way you have seen him go into heaven" (Acts 1:11, NIV).

In John 14:6, Jesus Himself said, "I will come again."

Did you know that one-third of the Bible deals with the topic of prophesy or end time events? That is a very large proportion of Scripture. Obviously, these events are important to God, and should be important to us as well.

Prophecy in Hindsight

Many of the prophecies in the pages of Scripture have already been fulfilled. For instance, so many of the predictions written about the coming of the Messiah are now part of history. Isaiah said He would be born of a virgin. Micah told us He would be born in the town of Bethlehem. Zechariah predicted He would be betrayed for thirty pieces of silver. Psalm 22 described His Roman crucifixion, hundreds of years before the rise of Rome, including the fact that His hands and feet would be pierced. Psalm 41 told of His betrayal by a close friend, and other Scriptures spoke of Him rising from the dead.

Psalm 22:1 even predicted the very words He would cry out from the cross as He was dying: "My God, My God, why have You forsaken Me?" The Bible very clearly predicted what the Messiah would do and how He would come, and those prophecies were all fulfilled to a "T."

But here's something very interesting: Even with all of those references to the Lord's first coming, the Bible refers five times more frequently to the *second* coming of Jesus Christ. For this reason, if we know He came the first time, which we do, we can be completely confident that He will also come the second time.

But when?

How soon?

Will He come in my lifetime?

I think He very well may, but no one can say with absolute certainty. Jesus Himself said: "But of that day and hour no one knows, not even the angels in heaven, nor the Son, but only the Father" (Mark 13:32).

In spite of this strong statement from the mouth of the Lord Himself, every now and then someone will pop up on the scene who claims to have figured out the day and the hour of Christ's coming (and wants you to buy his or her book to read all about it).

Don't ever be taken in by these claims. *No one* knows the time of our Lord's return. But if we can't know the day and the hour, the Bible does tell us that we can know "the times and the seasons" (1 Thessalonians 5:1). In other words, the Lord wants us to open our eyes to the fact that the time of His coming is, at last, drawing near.

You can see those signs on the front page of the newspaper, your news Website, or on your favorite news station on TV or radio. The headlines tell a story of a world feeling birth pains—pains arriving more and more frequently.

Iran (or fill in the blank) Threatens to Annihilate Israel.

China Builds up Military.

Another Shooting at School Kills 23.

America in Decline

Earthquake Rocks City. Thousands Feared Dead.

Signs, Signs, Signs

When you think about it, our life is really governed by signs. From the moment we get up in the morning, we're looking at signs. They flash at us from our iPhones, computer screens, or navigation screens in our cars. And then there are all those roadside signs. There's a red one shaped like an octagon with four letters on it. What does it mean? Judging by how people respond to it, it must mean "keep on rolling." There's another sign bearing the letters "S-L-O-W." What does that mean? Absolutely nothing to most people!

My wife and I went to visit a lady in the hospital not long, and while we were there I saw a sign I had never seen before. It had the image of an adult hand cradling a newborn baby, with the words "Safe Surrender Site." This was apparently a place where someone could safely deposit a newborn infant and simply walk away, no questions asked. It amazes me to see something like that—but it's better than a trash can or a dumpster, where many unwanted newborns are placed.

But that's a sign of the times, too. Paul told Timothy that in the last days people would be "without natural affection" (2 Timothy 3:3, KJV).

"Signs of the times," by the way, was the phrase coined by Jesus Himself in the book of Matthew.

> Then the Pharisees and Sadducees came, and testing Him asked that He would show them a sign from heaven. He answered and said to them, "When it is evening you say, 'It will be fair weather, for the sky is red'; and in the morning, 'It will be foul weather today, for the sky is red and threatening.' Hypocrites! You know how to discern the face of the sky, but you cannot discern the signs of the times. A wicked and adulterous generation seeks after a sign, and no sign shall be given to it except the sign of the prophet Jonah." And He left them and departed. (Matthew 16:1-4)

United in their hatred for Jesus, these two antagonistic groups of Jewish leaders came to test Jesus, demanding a miracle. That was a bit ironic, because Jesus had just been doing miracle after miracle—healing the sick, casting out demons, calming storms on the Sea of Galilee, feeding thousands of people from a little boy's lunch, and even raising someone from the dead.

And these guys needed a "sign"?

This demonstrates that no matter how many miracles some people witness, they will never allow their hearts to believe. To be specific, these Pharisees and Sadducees demanded that He show them a "sign from heaven." In Mark's gospel account of the same story, we're told that Jesus "sighed deeply."

I imagine that I would have sighed, too.

Have you ever had someone say something to you that was so

lame or off the wall that you couldn't even come up with a reply? Maybe all you could do was sigh, shake your head, or shrug your shoulders and walk away. That's how Jesus felt with these cold-hearted religious leaders. It's as though He was saying, *Oh come on. Really? Are you serious? After all I've done you're saying this to Me?* He knew very well they were just playing games, and didn't really want to believe.

He replied, in essence, "You guys do a great job at reading the weather signs, don't you? You look up at the clouds before you turn in for the night and predict what kind of day you're going to have tomorrow. But you can't see what is so plainly obvious, right before your very eyes."

It really doesn't take a genius to figure out what tomorrow's weather will look like. All I have to do is glance at the little app on my iPhone. If there's a little cartoon sun shining on my screen (par for the course in Southern California), then we'll enjoy great weather. If there's a rain cloud, then we may have a storm. Or, if I wanted to go low tech, I might step outside and look at the sky for a moment. Besides all that, bald men are always the first to know it's raining, when we feel that first little droplet of moisture on top of the head. That is sensitive instrumentation! My wife has so much hair she wouldn't know if it had been raining for a week!

So this isn't rocket science. You can see climate changes coming. And Jesus is saying, you guys do fine when it comes to playing amateur meteorologists, but you refuse to pay attention to the signs of the times right in front of your nose. You don't give a single serious thought about where you will spend eternity.

In the same way, there are people today who seem totally oblivious to the signs of the times. If I saw a woman who was obviously in her ninth month of pregnancy, I could be a prophet and predict she would soon give birth to a baby. (Especially is she was wearing one of those shirts with an arrow, that points down to the word "baby.")

Jesus was telling these leaders that they should open their eyes to the obvious. The signs of the times were all around them—as they are all around us, to an even greater degree.

Shrinking America ...

One such sign could include the diminishing stature of the United States of America as a superpower, and the emergence of other world powers in its place.

For years, students of biblical prophecy have wrestled with the question, "Where is the United States in the Bible's descriptions of last day events?" For whatever reason, America seems to be missing from the end-times scenario.

It makes you wonder. Why doesn't our nation seem to be one of the players at the end of history? While there are any number of theories that might be offered, we can certainly see this much: At the end of time, a new power emerges. We see the rise of the Antichrist, with ten nations confederated under him. We also see another mega-power called "the kings of the east," which will be able to field an army of 200 million. Sooner or later, this massive eastern army will face off with the Antichrist and his forces in the valley of Megiddo.

If you follow the news at all, you can't miss how strong China has emerged in recent days, both as an economic powerhouse and a military superpower. While other nations have moderated or cut defense spending, China continues to pour billions into its armaments and army. Experts are saying that within just a few years, China will overtake the United States as the world's top economy.

Another inescapable item in today's news is the push for a new world currency. In our own nation, there's a lot of talk about mandatory, high-tech national ID cards. These news accounts make Bible students sit up and take notice. They seem like a precursor to the "mark of the Beast," without which no one will be able to buy or sell.

Nevertheless, there is one ultra-clear "sign of the times" that outstrips all other in importance and significance.

I speak of the existence of the nation Israel.

The Biggest Sign of All

This isn't just a common road sign, it's like a massive billboard, with letters ten feet high.

When Israel declared its statehood on May 15, 1948, that event became the single greatest prophetic watersheds of our time. It's not just a sign of the times, it's a super sign. No nation been able to maintain its national identity even 300 to 500 years after being removed from its ancient homeland.

No nation except Israel.

With the perspective of history, we can now look back on scores of once great and powerful nations that now no longer exist. Think of the Hittites, a once mighty nation that grew into a vast empire. But where are they now? You don't hear a single thing about Hittites in the news. You can't pick up "Hittite Radio" on your satellite radio, and when the Olympic teams march into Olympic stadium in the opening ceremony of the games, no one carries the flag of the Hittites. There are no Hittite speed skate teams or high jumpers. Why? Because the Hittites effectively disappeared without a trace hundreds of years before the birth of Jesus.

The Jews, however, who were contemporaries of the Hittites, still exist as a people, and since 1948, as a nation.

A "sign of the times"?

Yes…a massive, miraculous sign.

As Israel's first prime minister, David Ben-Gurion, said, "If you know the story of Israel and what happened here and you do not believe in miracles you are not realistic. Something is wrong with you."[1]

Jesus said, "Now learn this parable from the fig tree: When its branch has already become tender and puts forth leaves, you know that summer is near. So you also, when you see all these things, know that it is near—at the doors!" (Matthew 24:32-33, NIV).

In Scripture the fig tree is a symbol of the nation Israel. Jesus is saying when you see the fig tree begin to bud again, you'll know that summer is near.

And so it is today. We can look around us and see "the buds on the fig tree." Spring is coming, with summer right behind. In other words, the signs of the times are telling that the coming of the Lord is drawing near.

Scripture is very specific about the scattering of the Jewish people to the four corners of the earth, and their eventual re-gathering.

> Say to them, 'This is what the Sovereign Lord says: I will take the Israelites out of the nations where they have gone. I will gather them from all around and bring them back into their own land. I will make them one nation in the land, on the mountains of Israel. There will be one king over all of them and they will never again be two nations or be divided into two kingdoms.' (Ezekiel 37:21-23, NIV)

Note the Lord's three major promises here: First, He says that He will take the people of Israel from among the nations where they have gone. Second, He will bring them to their own land. And third, He will make them into a nation again.

Have those things happened? Yes to all three!

When the Lord says these things, it's not like He is going out on a limb. Not at all! He knows the future better than you know the past. Would you think it amazing if I said to you, "I believe that such-and-such team won the World Series last fall"? No, that would be no big deal. I have recollection of the past. (Or I cheated and looked it up on my iPhone.)

Then again, if I picked who would win *next* year's World Series, you might say, "Lucky guess." But what if I predicted the teams and the final scores ten years from now…or fifty…or a hundred? I wouldn't be around to see some of those predictions fulfilled, but if I wrote them down, someone else would. And that's what God did—not just over a period of a decades or centuries, but thousands of years in advance.

Was He taking a risk? Of course not. God lives in the eternal realm and views the past, present, and future all in once glance. He sees everything. Knows everything.

Looking into the future of the Jewish race, God told the patriarch Abraham, "I will bless those who bless you, and I will curse those who curse you." And so it has been through history. Every nation that has risen up to strike Israel has paid the price. Egypt. Assyria. Babylon. Rome. And in more modern times Germany, Spain—and perhaps very soon Russia, if she is indeed the Magog force coming from the north of Israel spoken of in Scripture.

At least one nation has stood by modern Israel, and it is the United States of America. We were the first nation to acknowledge her statehood, and we have stood by her since that day. I firmly believe one of the reasons God has blessed our country is because we have blessed the nation Israel and the Jewish people. And when I see our country turning against with Israel, backing away from her, or siding with her enemies, I have very great concern.

There will come a time, however, when America will back away from Israel, and she will be left standing alone. That is when God will show His glory, and step in to defend her.

City of Peace?

Ironically the very name Jerusalem means "city of peace." Yet as we all know, it has been anything but a city of peace. More battles have been fought at the gates of Jerusalem than any other city on the face of the earth. And it shouldn't surprise anyone that she will find herself at the very center of the end times conflict.

I remember a statement from a presidential campaign years ago. Everyone kept saying, "It's the economy, stupid!" Nowadays, in current international politics, we could say, "It's Jerusalem, stupid."

Keep your eyes on Jerusalem…when the city's name pops into the headlines…when you hear about any new development taking place in or around this capital of Israel. Pay attention! Jerusalem is at the center of the storm—and will remain so—for one simple reason. She is claimed by two world religions, Judaism and Islam, as their own. Jerusalem is the city of the past, of the present, and of the future.

Jerusalem is a city of the past.

It became the capital of Israel under King David and was known as "the City of David." The first temple was built—and then rebuilt—in Jerusalem, and the glory of the Lord came to dwell in that place. Mount Moriah, now known as the temple mount, was where Abraham had been prepared to offer up his son Isaac as a burnt offering.

In that very same place—where the first and second temples had once stood—the Muslims believe that Mohammed ascended to heaven, and commemorated it by building a shrine there known as "the Dome of the Rock." As you might well imagine, there is unbelievable tension over that tiny slice of real estate.

Jerusalem is a city of the present.

After the modern state of Israel was declared in 1948, a war of independence left the city of Jerusalem divided, with Jordan retaining control over the old city, including the temple mount and most of the historic sites. During the Six Day War in 1967, however, when Israel's enemies united to attack her, Israelis were able to capture the old city and reunify all of Jerusalem. In that electrifying moment, Jerusalem fell under Jewish control for the first time in many centuries…and an astounding Bible prophesy came literally true.

Jerusalem is a city of the future.

The Bible declares that our world's final conflict will be in the Middle East, and centered around Jerusalem. Not around Paris. Not around Rome or London or New York City or Los Angeles, but Jerusalem. Zechariah 12 says,

> I will make Jerusalem and Judah like an intoxicating drink to all the nearby nations that send their armies to besiege Jerusalem. On that day I will make Jerusalem a heavy stone, a burden for the world. None of the nations who try to lift it will escape unscathed. (vv. 2-3, NLT)

That is why we watch with great interest what is happening in the Middle East—and why I am doing so now, even as I write these words. Will true democracies emerge out of the current bloodshed and turmoil…or will militant, radical groups like Al-Qaeda or the Muslim Brotherhood grab the ascendancy? A leader of the Egyptian Muslim Brotherhood, Kamal al-Halbawi, visited Tehran, and announced that he wanted a "true Islamic state" in his own country.

He went on to say that "Egypt should join a new world order with Iran and Venezuela plus Hezbollah and Hamas to chase away the Americans." He concluded his speech by saying that he goes to bed every night praying to Allah that he will wake up the next morning to see Israel "wiped off the face of the map". [2]

Iranian president Mahmoud Ahmadinejad, well known for his bellicose statements about destroying Israel, said in a speech, "Is it possible to have a world without the United States and Zionism? But you had best know that this slogan and this goal are attainable, and surely can be achieved. …The regime that is occupying Jerusalem must be eliminated from the pages of history."[3]

Why Jerusalem?

This ancient city is just the tiniest little speck on the globe. If you play with Google Earth on your computer and start zooming away from the city to see the whole Middle East—and the world—you can't help but notice what a miniscule, insignificant little city it is.

Yet the attention of the world remains riveted on it, just as God said it would be. And so it will be until the end.

It's a sign of the times.

It is also a wake-up call for those who claim the name of Jesus.

Chapter Two
MULTIPLYING SIGNS

"Tell us, when will this happen? What will be the signal for your coming and the end of the world?" —Matthew 24:3, Phillips

S ome signs, of course, are easier to read than others. This is especially true when you find yourself overseas, facing a language barrier. Things are often "lost in translation."

I remember being in England years ago and noticing signs in many of the windows that said, "BILL STICKERS WILL BE PROSECUTED." And I began to wonder, who is this Bill Stickers and what exactly has he done? Bill Stickers will be prosecuted? Why?

I finally asked someone and he said, "Oh, you're a bit of an idiot aren't you?" He told me that Bill Stickers are people who put posters up on walls and windows and such without asking permission. (Why didn't they just *say* so?)

Our team has also spent quite a bit of time in Australia, where I've encountered some interesting designations for certain foods. "Rocket," for instance, is a salad. And if it has shrimp in it, they call it *Bugs*. So you read in the menu "Rocket with Bugs." I said to the server, "What is this, exactly?" He explained it, but by that time I'd lost my appetite.

Even subtle changes in the language can throw you off a bit.

I came upon a collection of actual signs from around the world, written by non-English speakers attempting to use English words. The resulting message may fall a bit short of what the writer intended.

In a Bucharest hotel lobby, for instance, this sign was posted in front of the lift, or elevator: "The lift is being fixed for the next day. During that time we regret that you will be unbearable."

In a Paris hotel elevator, a sign read: "Please leave your values at the front desk."

In a Belgrade hotel elevator, another sign instructed: "To move the cabin push button for wishing floor. If the cabin should enter more persons each one should press a number of wishing floor. Driving is then going alphabetically by national order."

Okay….

A Hong Kong supermarket posted this notice: "For your convenience we recommend courageous efficient self-service." I kind of like that one. In a hotel in Athens, a notice proclaimed: "Visitors are expected to complain in the office between the hours of 9 and 11 daily." (No doubt they do, too.)

A dinner menu in a Polish hotel included this bizarre description of a certain dish. "Salad a firm's own make; Limpid red beet soup with cheesy dumplings in the form of a finger; Roasted duck let loose; Beef Rashers beaten up in the country people's fashion."

How about this one in an advertisement from a Hong Kong dentist? "Teeth extracted by the latest Methodists." Methodists pulling teeth in Hong Kong? Who would have known?

This one is kind of scary. In the window of a Swedish furrier, a sign read: "Fur coats made for ladies from their own skin." (I'm sure most English-speaking women would steer clear of that place!)

And did you hear about the detour sign in Japan that reads: "Stop. Drive sideways."

Or how about this one from a Copenhagen ticket office? "We take your bags and send them in all directions." (I can think of a number of airlines that could have adopted that motto.)

The truth is, some signs are clearer than others. Some are easy to read, and pretty straight-forward, while others are more difficult.

In the pages of the Bible, God has given us "signs of the times," if we will look for them. And these signs are telling us that Jesus Christ is coming again, and soon. (He says so Himself, by the way, in Revelation 22:20.)

What are some of these signs of the times?

The re-gathering of the nation Israel to its ancient homeland is a gigantic and unmistakable sign of His soon-coming. Linked closely to that important divine indicator is the Bible's warning that after the Jewish people have re-gathered in their homeland, their enemies will threaten to destroy them.

Anyone who follows the news, of course, will immediately think of Iran's ongoing threats to "wipe Israel off the map."

Speaking of watching the news, we can look around the world on any given day and watch as events unfold just as the Bible predicted they would in "the last days." What kinds of events? Things like global turmoil, an increase in earthquakes, tsunamis, the crash of the stock market, rapid changes in the global economy, the fading of the United States of America as the economic superpower, the rise of a united Europe, and the move toward a one-world currency.

Signs of the times.

Jesus told us that we are to be aware of the times and the seasons. In other words, to stay alert and keep our eyes open.

Truth for the Heart

It's one thing for people to be "interested in Bible prophecy" in an intellectual sort of way, trying to decipher names and places and events like some complex jigsaw puzzle. However, I think we need to approach this very significant subject with not only our minds, but also with our *hearts*. By that I mean we don't want to merely consider these things in an abstract academic way, but rather that we would allow God to move our hearts and change our behavior because of what we read. Someone has said that the Bible wasn't only written for our information or even our inspiration, but for our *transformation*.

When we read about the workings of God and the great events

just over the horizon, it ought to stir us, creating a sense of awe in our hearts. As God revealed to the prophet Daniel what was about to unfold in the future, the prophet dropped to his knees. He was stunned, and was unable to even speak. When he caught a glimpse of the future, it moved him to his very core.

It should be the same for us. In fact if we really understand what the Bible is saying about the imminent return of Jesus, it should cause us to want to live a more godly life. We read in 1 John 3:2–3, "Yes, dear friends, we are already God's children, and we can't even imagine what we will be like when Christ returns. But we do know that when he comes we will be like him, for we will see him as he really is. *And all who have this eager expectation will keep themselves pure, just as he is pure* (NLT).

In other words, if you really understand what the Bible is saying about the soon return of Jesus, it should cause you to want to live a pure, godly life. You should want to be on your toes, spiritually.

Some might say, "You know, I've never really understood all of that Bible prophecy stuff. Antichrist this. Millennium that. Rapture. Mid-Trib, Post-Trib. I don't know what it means. I can't sort it out. I'll just let the experts figure those things out."

That may be an understandable response to confusion over details about prophetic teaching, but we really don't want to ignore what the Bible has to say about these things. In fact, there is a special blessing promised for those who would hear and keep the words of this prophecy.

> Blessed is he who reads and those who hear the words of this prophecy, and keep those things which are written in it; for the time is near. (Revelation 1:3)

You want to be blessed, don't you? What is true about the study of the book of Revelation is no doubt true in principle as we look at what all of the Bible teaches about end times events.

The fact is, God must have wanted us to learn Bible prophecy, because at least thirty percent of the Scriptures are dedicated to this topic. And God wants us to know and understand that He keeps His Word. Just as surely as He kept His Word with prophesies that foretold the arrival of the Messiah in Bethlehem, He wants us to know He will keep His Word about the prophesies pertaining to the return of the Messiah.

Tim LaHaye, who has written extensively on the topic of Bible prophecy, makes this statement: "No scholar of academic substance denies that Jesus lived almost 2,000 years ago. And yet we find three times as many prophecies in the Bible relating to His Second Coming as to His first. Thus the Second Advent of our Lord is three times as certain as His first coming, which can be verified as historical fact."[4]

A World in Turmoil

When Jesus described the world prior to His second coming, He painted a picture of a planet stirred by strife, war, suffering, and famine in the midst of plenty, rocked by great earthquakes, and ravished by pestilence. Luke 21 tells us: "And there will be strange signs in the sun, moon, and stars. And here on earth the nations will be in turmoil, perplexed by the roaring seas and strange tides. People will be terrified at what they see coming upon the earth, for the powers in the heavens will be shaken (NLT).

Another translation puts it this way. "It will seem like all hell has broken loose—sun, moon, stars, earth, sea, in an uproar and everyone all over the world in a panic, the wind knocked out of them by the threat of doom, the powers-that-be quaking." (Luke 21:25-26, THE MESSAGE).

The Bible tells us that prior to the return of Christ to the earth, there will be an increase in earthquakes. Luke 21:11 says, "There will be great earthquakes, famines and pestilences in various places, and fearful events and great signs from heaven" (NIV).

Of course, we have always had earthquakes…and tsunamis and hurricanes. But there is no doubt that all of these have dramatically increased in recent years. For the past five decades, every decade has seen an increase in the number of earthquakes—and not minor quakes, either. According to Hal Lindsey, they are *killer* quakes coming at a level and a frequency like we have never seen before.[5]

A recent quake in China claimed the lives of at least 69,000 people. In 2005, an earthquake in Pakistan sent 80,000 people into eternity. And news of the massive quake in Haiti, still in the news as I write these words, has taken the lives of over 200,000 men, women, and children.

Many of us remember the catastrophic tsunami of December 26, 2004, caused by the fourth most powerful undersea earthquake on record. It was an earthquake that was so powerful it moved the entire island of Sumatra 100 feet to the southwest from its pre-quake position. And in that particular earthquake and tsunami, 290,000 people lost their lives.

Jesus told us, "You will see an increase in earthquakes." We have, and that is a "sign of the times" that is difficult to miss. Jesus describes these devastating events as birth pangs or labor pains. And He goes on to say that these are merely the beginning of birth pangs.[6]

In the same way, Jesus indicates that national disasters will begin to increase in frequency and intensity shortly before His return. These things are reminders—for all who are willing to receive them—that Christ is coming back again.

A Quick Fly-Over

As we prepare to dig into these things, let me set forth what I believe to be a chronology of the major end times events. This will just be a quick flyover, and we'll come back later and fill in some of the gaps.

In my opinion, the next event on the prophetic calendar is what the Bible describes as *the rapture of the church*. This is spoken of in the book of 1 Thessalonians, the fourth chapter, where we read:

> But I do not want you to be ignorant, brethren, concerning those who have fallen asleep, lest you sorrow as others who have no hope. For if we believe that Jesus died and rose again, even so God will bring with Him those who sleep in Jesus.
>
> For this we say to you by the word of the Lord, that we who are alive

and remain until the coming of the Lord will by no means precede those who are asleep. For the Lord Himself will descend from heaven with a shout, with the voice of an archangel, and with the trumpet of God. And the dead in Christ will rise first. Then we who are alive and remain shall be caught up together with them in the clouds to meet the Lord in the air. And thus we shall always be with the Lord. (vv. 13-17)

The term "rapture" comes from the Latin word *rapturus*, which means "taken by force." In this instance, it means we will be caught up to meet the Lord in the air, and then we will be with Him forever.

Jesus, talking about this same event, said, "I tell you, in that night there will be two men in one bed: the one will be taken and the other will be left. Two women will be grinding together: the one will be taken and the other left. Two men will be in the field: the one will be taken and the other left." (Luke 17:34-36) Paul says this of this event, the rapture, that it will happen "in a moment, in the twinkling of an eye."[7]

I believe that either right before or right after the rapture, a large force from the north, known as "Magog" in Scripture, will attack the nation of Israel. Shortly thereafter, a man will emerge on the scene that the Bible describes as "the beast" and "the Antichrist."

Don't let that word "beast" fool you. He will be smooth, charismatic, skillful, and a marvelous communicator. He will come with economic solutions that will amaze everyone, and with a peace treaty that the Arab nations and the Jews will both actually sign. And he will come with promises of great peace. In fact, he will be heralded by some as the very messiah.

His very title, however, Antichrist, gives you an indication as to who he truly is. The prefix "anti," of course, means *against*, or *instead of*. Many will hail him as the world's savior because of what he will be able to accomplish in such a short time.

So the Antichrist will come as a man of peace. He will do away with the monetary system as we know it today, and no one will be able to buy or sell without his mark. At the halfway point of the seven-year period known as the Tribulation, he will show his true colors, and something called "the abomination of desolation" will take place. This will occur after the third Jewish temple has been rebuilt in Israel, and the Antichrist erects an image of himself and commands worship.

This is a significant point of the Tribulation period, and we read about God's judgments beginning to fall upon the earth. The Antichrist begins a campaign of intense persecution against Christians and Jews, and various events unfold that ultimately culminate in the final battle known as the Battle of Armageddon, fought in the valley of Megiddo in Israel. During that climactic battle, Jesus Christ Himself returns to the earth in what we know as the Second Coming.

In the rapture He comes *for* His church, and we are caught up to meet the Lord in the air. In the Second Coming, He comes *with* His church as He returns to earth. And then the Millennium begins. Millennium means "a thousand," and what follows is a thousand year reign of Christ over this earth. During this glorious period, Satan will be chained up, and unable to wreak havoc on the earth. At the end of the Millennium, Satan will be released briefly in a final rebellion. After he is defeated for the final time, he is cast into the lake of fire forever. And then New Jerusalem comes down from heaven to earth, and heaven and earth effectively become one. This will be the ultimate fulfillment of what our Lord taught us in the Lord's Prayer when He said, "Your kingdom come, Your will be done on earth as it is in heaven."[8]

Sometimes you hear people say, "After I die, I will go to heaven and be there forever with the Lord." That is not totally true. You *will* be with the Lord forever, but one day heaven and earth will become one. There will be a new earth.

So this is an overview of things to come, and you can be certain that events will unfold exactly as the Bible has said.

"Take Heed..."

In the gospel of Mark, we read these words:

> Then as He went out of the temple, one of His disciples said to Him, "Teacher, see what manner of stones and what buildings are here!"

> And Jesus answered and said to him, "Do you see these great buildings? Not one stone shall be left upon another, that shall not be thrown down."

> Now as He sat on the Mount of Olives opposite the temple, Peter, James, John, and Andrew asked Him privately, "Tell us, when will these things be? And what will be the sign when all these things will be fulfilled?"

> And Jesus, answering them, began to say: "Take heed that no one deceives you. For many will come in My name, saying, 'I am He,' and will deceive many. But when you hear of wars and rumors of wars, do not be troubled; for such things must happen, but the end is not yet. For nation will rise against nation, and kingdom against kingdom. And there will be earthquakes in various places, and there will be famines and troubles. These are the beginnings of sorrows."

> ...For in those days there will be tribulation, such as has not been since the beginning of the creation which God created until this time, nor ever shall be. And unless the Lord had shortened those days, no flesh would be saved; but for the elect's sake, whom He chose, He shortened the days.

> "Then if anyone says to you, 'Look, here is the Christ!' or, 'Look, He is there!' do not believe it. For false christs and false prophets will rise and show signs and wonders to deceive, if possible, even the elect. But take heed; see, I have told you all things beforehand."
> (Mark 13:1-8, 19-23)

What Christ has just described is the Tribulation period. When He talks about, "Many will come in My name saying, 'I am Christ,' and deceive many," He is not only talking about false prophets but He is also talking about the Antichrist himself. The events of the Tribulation period are like a group of dominoes stacked closely together. And when the first one falls, the rest will fall after. You have the Antichrist, then you have war, earthquakes, and on it goes. So what we are seeing now in this present time—a "killer quake here," another war breaking out there—are just glimpses of things to come.

Jesus reminds us, however, that as the time draws near, we will see an increase in the frequency of these shocking events. And when we see these things, we can know that we are getting closer and closer to the time of the Tribulation period and to the end of the world as we know it. But today's headlines, terrible as they may be, are just a small foretaste of what is to come.

Temple Talk

The backdrop for the conversation captured above in Mark 13 was the disciples pointing out the magnificent Jewish temple. They were saying, "Just look at this marvelous temple, Lord. How magnificent it is! What do you think about that?"

The Lord's reply shocked them out of their sandals. The temple that so enthralled and amazed them would soon be a pile of rubble, with not one stone left standing upon another.

This was the second Jewish temple, being constructed by Herod at that point, and it had been under construction for forty-six years. In fact, it was destroyed just seven short years after it was finally completed. But while it lasted, it was certainly a magnificent structure.

If you look at the skyline of Jerusalem today you will notice a building with a large gold dome on the top. That is known as the Dome of the Rock, and that is not what the disciples were looking at. In that day, a mighty temple stood on that site, with massive walls of huge stones and sheets of gold that flashed and glowed as the sun set over Jerusalem each night. It was considered one of the wonders of the ancient world, and it's certainly no surprise that the disciples would have been so impressed by it.

Jesus, however, made a radical and specific prediction: "I say unto you, not one stone shall be left upon another."

Did the prediction come true?

Yes, it did, and exactly as He described it. Just decades after He shocked His followers with that prophecy, in A.D. 70, the Roman general Titus built large wooden scaffolds on that same temple, piled them high with wood and flammable items, and set them on fire. The heat from that fire was intense that the gold on the temple melted in between the crevices. As a result, the Romans dismantled the gutted building stone by stone to retrieve the gold.

The prophecy was fulfilled exactly as Jesus had said. In fact, that is one of the many reasons why you can place trust and confidence in the truths of the Bible. Because the Bible is the one book that dares to predict the future again and again and again with perfect accuracy.

Significance of Israel

One of the most vital things we need to understand as we look at Bible prophecy is the significance of the nation Israel. In Mark 13, Jesus compares the nation to a fig tree.

> Now learn this parable from the fig tree: When its branch has already become tender, and puts forth leaves, you know that summer is near. So you also, when you see these things happening, know that it is near—at the doors! Assuredly, I say to you, this generation will by no means pass away till all these things take place. Heaven and earth will pass away, but My words will by no means pass away. (vv. 28-31)

This comparison of Israel with a fig tree happens several times in Scripture. In Hosea 9:10, the Lord says, "I found Israel like grapes in the wilderness; I saw your fathers as the firstfruits on the fig tree in its first season."

Scripture makes similar comparisons in Judges 9 and Joel 1.

So here is what Jesus is saying: The rebirth of the nation Israel isn't just a sign of the last days, it is a *super* sign of the last days.

The Bible is specifically saying the Jews will be re-gathered in their ancient homeland of Israel once again.

Let's consider a brief history of the Jewish people. Her roots go back to Abraham, when God established a covenant with him and with his descendents. In Genesis 17 we read that

> When Abram was ninety-nine years old, the LORD appeared to Abram and said to him, 'I am Almighty God; walk before Me and

be blameless. And I will make My covenant between Me and you, and will multiply you exceedingly.... And I will establish My covenant between Me and you and your descendants after you in their generations, for an everlasting covenant, to be God to you and your descendants after you. Also I give to you and your descendants after you the land in which you are a stranger, all the land of Canaan, as an everlasting possession; and I will be their God. (vv. 1-2, 7-8)

The Lord is very specific in saying to Abraham that the land of Canaan, later to be conquered by the Hebrew people, would be their land forever. That "land of Canaan" is essentially modern day Israel, though at this time they don't occupy all of the land originally given to them by the Lord.

Not only did God promise this land to His people, but He also made this profound statement in Genesis 12:

I will make you a great nation;
I will bless you
And make your name great;
And you shall be a blessing.
I will bless those who bless you,
And I will curse him who curses you;
And in you all the families of the earth shall be blessed.
(vv. 2-3)

God has blessed the world through the Jewish people. It is through the Jews that our Bible came. It is through the Jews that our Messiah came. And God has promised that those who would bless Israel and bless the Jewish people would be blessed of God, while those who cursed Israel and cursed the Jewish people would be cursed by God.

If you don't believe that promise is true, just pull out your history books. Look at every nation that has tried to destroy the Jews, and how God has dealt with them. I believe one of the reasons the Lord has so richly blessed the United States of America is because of our support for the nation of Israel. He has blessed us because we have blessed them, and if we begin to curtail or withdraw our support, it would be a monumental mistake.

Israel is the only true democracy in that part of the world, but even more than that, Israel is a nation specifically established by God Himself. They are still His people, and He has a plan for them in the future.

This is not a political issue, but rather a *scriptural* issue that we're dealing with here.

So God made a covenant with Abraham, with his son, Isaac, and with Isaac's son, Jacob. Jacob had a son named Joseph, and you may remember the story of how his brothers sold him into slavery. Through a remarkable series of circumstances, Joseph not only ended up in Egypt, but as the second most powerful man in all of Egypt, and was placed in charge of that nation's food supply. When a famine hit the land, Joseph's brothers, along with their father Jacob, made their way to Egypt to receive food from Joseph's own hand.

Fast-forwarding 400 years, the Jews had multiplied greatly, and Pharaoh was using them for slave labor. In fact, there were so many Jews in that land that he felt threatened by their numbers, and began devising ways to thin their ranks. It began with a decree that every newborn Hebrew baby boy should be killed outright. Through God's providence, however, one of those baby boys was placed in a waterproofed basket, and set down in the Nile River where Pharaoh's daughter came to bathe. When she found the child, she took him into her home as her own.

This little boy, of course, was Moses. According to the Jewish historian, Josephus, he was being groomed to become the next Pharaoh of Egypt. But Moses, being a Jew, saw the plight of his fellow Hebrews. God directed him to bring about their deliverance and the great Exodus took place, when all the Jews left Egypt, and made their way across wilderness to the Promised Land.

It took them forty years to get there, of course. Some have said it's because men were in charge, and they wouldn't stop to ask for directions! But that's not true. The real reason for their long wanderings and going in circles was because of their disobedience to the Lord.

Eventually, however, they came to the Promised Land. Moses died just before they crossed over into Canaan, and Joshua led them in and they conquered this new land, just as God had said they would.

The promise of Abraham was fulfilled: They were in the land, and it was theirs.

Through the years, however, the Hebrew people turned away from the Lord, and began giving their devotion and worship to man-made idols. Speaking through His prophets, God pleaded with the people to turn away from this corrupting sin, before it destroyed them. But again and again they hardened their hearts and refused. Even when the Lord warned them that another nation would overtake them, destroy their cities, and take them as slaves, they still refused to listen.

Finally, because God's rebellious people would seemingly have it no other way, they were conquered by King Nebuchadnezzar, and the Israelites who weren't killed outright were taken into captivity to Babylon for seventy years. At the end of the seventy years, the Jews returned to Israel and Jerusalem and began to rebuild on the ashes and the ruins.

Centuries later, when the nation was occupied by Rome, the long-awaited Messiah of Israel finally stepped onto the scene. For the most part, however, He was rejected by His own people. As the Scripture says, "He was in the world, and the world was made through Him, and the world did not know Him. He came to His own, and His own did not receive Him" (John 1:10-11).

Denounced and betrayed, Jesus was arrested by Rome, crucified on a cross, and rose again on the third day and ascended to His Father in heaven. Not many years after that, the Jewish people in the land rebelled against their Roman overlords. General Titus overcame Jerusalem, destroyed their city, burned down their second temple, and effectively scattered them to the four corners of the earth.

No Ordinary Nation

It is abundantly clear that if this had been an ordinary nation under ordinary circumstances, that would have been the end of it. No more Israel. No more national identity. Not now, not ever.

But Israel is not and never will be "an ordinary nation."

For all of their wandering and rebellion through the years, the Jewish people remain (to this day) the very apple of God's eye. In His Word God had promised that, scattered as the Jewish people may have been, they would one day return to their homeland, and the nation would be reborn.

They did, and it was.

On May 14, 1948, the last British forces left Haifa, and the Jewish Agency, led by David Ben-Gurion, declared the State of Israel, in accordance with the 1947 UN Partition Plan. Both superpower leaders, U.S. President Harry S. Truman, and Soviet leader Joseph Stalin, immediately recognized the new state.[9]

Super sign?

What else could you call it? Such a thing could have never, ever happened apart from the mighty hand of a sovereign God. He said He would take the sons of Israel from among the nations where they had gone, gathering them from every side, and bringing them into their own land as a nation.

And that's just what He has done.

After World War II and the horrific events of the Holocaust, Jews began to return to their homeland, and we are seeing the prophecy of Ezekiel and others fulfilled before our very eyes.

Since that day in 1948 when Israel once again became a nation, the prophetic clock has been ticking. Will the end come in our generation? Jesus said: "I tell you the truth, this generation will certainly not pass away until all these things have happened" (Matthew 24:34, NIV).

How Should These Things Affect Us?

As I've already noted, the study of Bible prophecy is more than just an interesting pastime or an academic exercise. God didn't record these things for us to sit back and say, "Well, now, isn't that interesting?" No, He gave us these prophecies to change our lives. So what should we do in light of what we have just seen? Three things:

We should wake up.

We should sober up.

We should suit up.

In 1 Thessalonians chapter 5, the apostle Paul writes:

> So then, let us not be like others, who are asleep, but let us be alert and sober. For those who sleep, sleep at night, and those who get drunk, get drunk at night. But since we belong to the day, let us be sober, putting on faith and love as a breastplate, and the hope of salvation as a helmet. (vv. 6-8, NIV)

The teaching of Christ's return is a litmus test of where you are at spiritually. If you are walking with God and enjoying His presence every day, hearing that Jesus could come back at any time will motivate and excite you. That knowledge will continue to nudge you to live with integrity and purity. Why? Because you want to be right with God. For the person who is not right with God, however, hearing that Jesus may appear at any moment is a frightening and alarming prospect.

Here again, then, is how the apostle Paul urges us to live in light of Christ's soon coming.

#1 We Need to Wake Up

Paul says in verse 6, "Let us not be like others, who are asleep." There are people today who are asleep in the church.

The truth is, people fall asleep in church all the time. Not just physically but spiritually, too. You may hear the Word of God, but because you never put it to work in your life, you become spiritually lethargic. Or maybe you become a "spiritual connoisseur," with all sorts of critical comments to make about the pastor, the sermon, or the church service.

Hmm, well, I don't think that message was quite as good as the one two weeks ago. And I really like Pastor X better than Pastor Y....

No, we should let the truths of God's Word move us—move us to obey, move us to action, move us into a closer relationship with God. "Wake up!" the Bible is saying. "The signs of the times are all around you, and Jesus Christ is coming back again."

Does that thought bring you joy and a sense of anticipation? Does it make your heart beat just a little bit faster? C. H. Spurgeon put it this way:

It is a very blessed thing to be on the watch for Christ. It is a blessing to us now. It detaches you from the world. You can be poor without murmuring. You can be rich without worldliness. You can be sick without sorrowing. You can be healthy without presumption. If you are always waiting for Christ's coming untold blessings are wrapped up in that glorious hope.[10]

So we need to wake up.

#2 We Need to Sober Up

Verse 8 says, "But since we belong to the day, let us be sober."

When I was growing up, I spent a lot of time around intoxicated people. For seventeen years of my life, I was in an alcoholic home, where I witnessed people getting drunk from morning until night.

As a result, I observed all kinds of people and the way that they react to alcohol. I've noticed that when many people get "under the influence," they try to act as though they are not under the influence. Invariably, however, they give themselves away.

One of the principal ways that police officers nail people who are driving while intoxicated is by observing those who are driving too slowly, as well as those driving too fast. You'll see someone in the fast lane doing twenty miles an hour. That's usually a DUI, and sooner or later, he or she will get caught at it.

Jesus said in Luke 21, "Be careful, or your hearts will be weighed down with dissipation, drunkenness and the anxieties of life, and that day will close on you unexpectedly like a trap" (v. 34, NIV).

To be sober means that you are clear-headed. You are to be alert, sane, and steady, with your eyes open. Don't be drunk or careless, and don't let yourself be preoccupied or overcome with cares and worries. Be awake and alert.

#3 We Need to Suit Up

1 Thessalonians 5:8 continues, saying, "…putting on the breastplate of faith and love, and as a helmet the hope of salvation."

This is the specific instruction from the apostle, that we are to put our armor on in these days. My friend, we are in a spiritual battle. It's war! And if you fail to realize this or prepare for this, you're in danger of becoming a casualty. One of the signs of the end times is that people will fall away from the faith, giving heed to seducing spirits and the doctrines that demons teach.[11] There has never been a time where it is more important for us to know our Bibles and to walk closely with God. As our world draws nearer and nearer to its final curtain, there will be more and more false teaching and various vices that are designed to entrap you and pull you away from God. We need to be sane, clear-headed, and alert to the fact that Christ could come back at any time.

Wake up. Sober up, and suit up.

In the Phillips translation of Romans 13, Paul writes:

Why all this stress on behaviour? Because, as I think you have realised, the present time is of the highest importance—it is time to wake up to reality. Every day brings God's salvation nearer. The night is nearly over, the day has almost dawned. Let us therefore fling away the things that men do in the dark, let us arm ourselves for the fight of the day! Let us live cleanly, as in the daylight, not in the "delights" of getting drunk or playing with sex, nor yet in quarrelling or jealousies. Let us be Christ's men from head to foot, and give no chances to the flesh to have its fling. (vv. 11-14)

Are you ready for His return?

You say, "Well, how do you know if you are ready?"

It all boils down to this: You know you are ready if you have a relationship with Jesus Christ, if you are walking daily with Him, and if you are watching and waiting for His return. The understanding of Christ's imminent return should cause you to want to live a godly life and be as ready as you can be. You don't have to be perfect. No one is. But you need to be prepared and ready.

Are you?

Chapter Three
ANTI-CHRIST, AMERICA & ARMAGEDDON

Dear children, this is the last hour; and as you have heard that the antichrist is coming, even now many antichrists have come. This is how we know it is the last hour.
—*1 John 2:18*, NIV

The Antichrist generates a lot of interest among Christians and non-Christians alike.

Hollywood has featured him in a number of movies, including *Rosemary's Baby*, *The Devil's Advocate*, *The Omen*, and another recently released film simply called *The Antichrist*. Singer Marilyn Manson dedicated an entire album to him, calling it "Antichrist Superstar." Google his name and you will generate almost five million pages.

Many people are fascinated by this mysterious figure, whose emergence on the modern scene was prophesied thousands of years ago.

His aliases include: the Man of Sin, the Son of Perdition, the Little Horn, the Wicked One, and the Prince Who is to Come.

Who is this man? What will he be like?

Personally, I don't think he'll be anything like what we expect. He won't be dressed in all black with glowing red eyes and steam rising from his back. He won't stride onto the world scene with the Darth Vader theme playing in the background.

I think this man will be suave, intelligent, well-read, engaging, magnetic, and charismatic. He will probably be well-dressed, and might very well grace the cover of *Time* magazine, as well as *GQ*.

Maybe so.

Yet no matter what he looks like or how he comes across, the man will be the most wicked individual who has ever walked the face of the earth. If Satan ever had a son, it would be this person that we call the Antichrist.

And by the way, most Americans believe such a man is coming. In a *US News and World Report* article some years ago, a poll stated that 49 percent of Americans believe there will be an Antichrist sometime in the future.[12] Then in a *Newsweek* poll, 19 percent of Americans said they believe the Antichrist is on earth right now.[13]

You might be surprised to know that the Bible has quite a lot to say about this individual. There are at least a hundred passages of Scripture describing the origin, nationality, character, career, kingdom, and final doom of the Antichrist.

From what I can surmise from my study of Scripture and how those truths correlate with today's events, I believe we are close to seeing the events of the end times begin unfolding right before our eyes.

Some will say, "Oh come off it, Greg. I've heard that kind of talk for years." Yes, and so have I. Be that as it may, there has never been such a unique alignment of events—along with the latest breakthroughs in technology—that could actually produce the scenario we'll be considering in the following pages of this chapter.

And bear in mind that it isn't only Bible-believing evangelicals who see this pattern taking shape. In fact, there is a group of scientists—including eighteen Nobel Laureates—who get together and vote periodically on how close they believe we are to the end of the world.

The so-called Doomsday Clock is a symbolic clock face, maintained since 1947 by the board of directors of the *Bulletin of the Atomic Scientists* at the University of Chicago. The closer the clock is to midnight, the closer the world is estimated to be to global disaster. Since its creation, the time on the clock has changed nineteen times. As of January 14, 2010, the Doomsday Clock now stands at six minutes to midnight.[14]

Why do they believe this? Because they are aware of the fact that there are 27,000 nuclear weapons on the face of the earth today—and not all of them are possessed by the so-called super powers. Nuclear weapons are now within the grasp of rogue nations like North Korea and Iran, who threaten on a regular basis to actually *use* these weapons of mass destruction to further their evil aims.

Then they add the possibility of one of these nukes ending up in the hands of a terrorist group—who no doubt would use them, and you have a frightening scenario indeed.

So What Will Happen Next?

I believe the next event on the prophetic calendar will be the rapture of the church. In fact, some of the events we will read about in the next few pages could not even unfold until after the rapture has taken place. I don't believe the Antichrist will emerge onto the world scene until the church is removed.

Why do I say this? One big reason is because of what I read in 2 Thessalonians 2:7–9:

> For the mystery of lawlessness is already at work; only He who now restrains will do so until He is taken out of the way. And then the lawless one will be revealed, whom the Lord will consume with the breath of His mouth and destroy with the brightness of His coming.

I believe "the lawless one" refers to the Antichrist, and "He who restrains" refers to the work of the Holy Spirit through the church. In other words, godly, Christ-loving men and women are part of that restraining force in these days in which we live. People who speak out against what is wrong, and fearlessly declare what is right. But once we are removed from this planet through the rapture, then this wicked one—the beast, the Antichrist—can quickly be revealed, and will step out onto the world stage.

There is no point in trying to figure out who this Antichrist might be. You won't be able to. No one will. The fact is, the Bible doesn't tell us to be watching for the Antichrist, but rather to be looking for *Jesus Christ* Himself! Our focus and our attention in these turbulent times need to be totally on Him. Hebrews 9:28 tells us: "Christ was sacrificed once to take away the sins of many people; and he will appear a second time, not to bear sin, but to bring salvation to those who are waiting for him" (NIV).

Jesus said, "Now when these things begin to happen, look up and lift up your heads, because your redemption draws near" (Luke 21:28).

That doesn't mean we're all supposed to stand out on street corners and stare up into the sky like a bunch of idiots. To "look up" means to live with a sense of anticipation and in a state of readiness. We need to be ready to go at any time, because the Lord will come for His own, and snatch us away in the twinkling of an eye.

Nevertheless, the Antichrist is close.

And if he is close, then the coming of Jesus is even closer.

Kept from the Hour of Trial

I do not believe that the Church, those who belong to Jesus Christ, will be left to go through the horrendous period of time known in Scripture as the Great Tribulation. In Revelation 3:10, the Lord says to the church: "Since you have kept my command to endure patiently, I will also keep you from the hour of trial that is going to come upon the whole world to test those who live on the earth" (NIV).

In other words, the Lord is saying, "Because you have persevered, because you have stayed close to me, I'm going to keep you from this hour of trial, this hour of tribulation."

Now some might say, "Wait a second. Doesn't the Bible say, 'In this world you will have tribulation'?" Yes it does. But there is a big difference between personal troubles and trials and what the Bible describes as the Great Tribulation period. Obviously, we all go through deep waters and have to endure hardships, disappointments, and tragedies in our lives. But these heartaches and trials can't really be compared to that seven-year period of human history when God's white-hot wrath will be poured out on a world that has rejected His Son.

Why do I believe the Church won't go through this specific period of wrath and judgment? Because you won't find any precedent for such a thing in Scripture.

I think the apostle Peter himself makes one of the greatest defenses for a pre-tribulation rapture when he points out in his second letter that God spared Noah and his family, getting them safely into the ark before the flood came. He also cites the example of Lot, who was delivered from Sodom and Gomorrah before the judgment came upon those evil cities. And then Peter concludes in 2 Peter 2:9, "The Lord knows how to deliver the godly out of temptations and to reserve the unjust under punishment for the day of judgment."

We are also told in 1 Thessalonians 5:9, "For God did not appoint us to suffer wrath but to receive salvation through our Lord Jesus Christ" (NIV).

For these reasons and more, I don't believe the Great Tribulation can begin until after the Church has been removed from the scene.

After the church is raptured, then, after we are caught up in the twinkling of an eye to meet the Lord in the air and we are reunited with our loved ones…then what?

Then the Antichrist emerges.

Let's take a closer look at the description of him that we are given in the sixth chapter of the book of Revelation.

The Unveiling

Revelation 6 is an *unveiling*—which is literally what the word "revelation" means. In the pages of this last book of the Bible, we have the unveiling of human history. Chapter six gives us a bird's eye view of those events—especially the Great Tribulation—as illustrated by the four horsemen of the apocalypse.

> Now I saw when the Lamb opened one of the seals; and I heard one of the four living creatures saying with a voice like thunder, "Come and see." And I looked, and behold, a white horse. He who sat on it had a bow; and a crown was given to him, and he went out

conquering and to conquer.

When He opened the second seal, I heard the second living creature saying, "Come and see." Another horse, fiery red, went out. And it was granted to the one who sat on it to take peace from the earth, and that people should kill one another; and there was given to him a great sword.

When He opened the third seal, I heard the third living creature say, "Come and see." So I looked, and behold, a black horse, and he who sat on it had a pair of scales in his hand. And I heard a voice in the midst of the four living creatures saying, "A quart of wheat for a denarius, and three quarts of barley for a denarius; and do not harm the oil and the wine."

When He opened the fourth seal, I heard the voice of the fourth living creature saying, "Come and see." So I looked, and behold, a pale horse. And the name of him who sat on it was Death, and Hades followed with him. And power was given to them over a fourth of the earth, to kill with sword, with hunger, with death, and by the beasts of the earth.

When He opened the fifth seal, I saw under the altar the souls of those who had been slain for the word of God and for the testimony which they held. And they cried with a loud voice, saying, "How long, O Lord, holy and true, until You judge and avenge our blood on those who dwell on the earth?" Then a white robe was given to each of them; and it was said to them that they should rest a little while longer, until both the number of their fellow servants and their brethren, who would be killed as they were, was completed. (Revelation 6:1-11)

The First Horseman

The tribulation period begins with the emergence of the white horse or the Antichrist. Some have mistakenly thought that the rider of the white horse, the first of the four horsemen portrayed here in Revelation 6, is a reference to Christ Himself. But it isn't. This is the Antichrist. Why does the description sound similar to a description of Jesus? Because that's the Antichrist's method of operation.

He is an *imitator*. A pale version of the real thing. He seeks to appear to be like Christ, and quite frankly, some will think he is the

Christ. In a parallel passage in Matthew 24 that closely follows Revelation 6, Jesus declared, "Many will come in My name saying, 'I am Christ.'"[15]

The Antichrist will deceive many because he will be a "man of peace." He'll be a charismatic leader, a gifted orator, and an individual who will persuade old enemies and warring parties to finally lay down their suspicions and their arms and sign agreements. He will even get Israel and the Arab nations to sign a peace treaty, paving the way for the long-awaited third temple. No diplomat, president, king, or prime minister has ever been able to pull this off before, but the Antichrist will break new ground, and many will be awed and amazed by his abilities.

There have certainly been any number of signed agreements in the Middle East, but none of them ever last. The parties may sign a peace treaty in the morning, but they'll be fighting before lunch. *But where others have failed, the Antichrist will succeed.* In fact, his accomplishments will be so spectacular in the eyes of some—so far-reaching and unprecedented—that many will hail him as the very Messiah. The Christ.

I was speaking with an Israeli man awhile back and we were talking about Messiah. As with most Israelis, he didn't believe that Jesus is the Messiah, as Christians do.

"Well," I asked him, "who do you believe the Messiah will be?"

"I believe the messiah will be a man of peace," he replied. "And when he comes, he'll help us rebuild our temple, and he will bring a peace agreement."

"Sir," I replied, "you just described the Antichrist."

"Call him what you like," he said. "*He* will be our messiah."

It's perfectly understandable how the Jewish people living in their homeland long for peace. They've had war for generations, and they don't want any more. They're just trying to defend their borders and live normal lives, without the shadow of threats, terrorism, and attacks on innocent civilians.

So can you imagine how many Israelis will respond when a man comes along who seems able to actually get that done—to obtain a Middle-East peace agreement where so many have failed before? That's why he'll be thought of as the very Messiah of God.

The Bible, however, tells us who he really is.

Scripture describes him in a number of different ways. One of those descriptions is "the man of sin." In 2 Thessalonians 2:3, Paul writes: "Don't let anyone deceive you in any way, for that day will not come until the rebellion occurs and the man of lawlessness is revealed, the man doomed to destruction. He will oppose and will exalt himself over everything that is called God or is worshiped, so that he sets himself up in God's temple, proclaiming himself to be God" (NIV).

The Antichrist will be history's vilest embodiment of sin and rebellion. He is also called "the man of lawlessness."

> Then the man of lawlessness will be revealed, whom the Lord Jesus will consume with the breath of his mouth and destroy by the splendor of his coming. (2 Thessalonians 2:8)

He will oppose every law of God. He will not only be against Christ, but he will also come offering himself in the place of Christ. And as he becomes entrenched in power, he will show himself to be a bloodthirsty world dictator that would make Mao Tse-Tung, Adolf Hitler, Joseph Stalin, Saddam Hussein, and Osama bin Laden look like lightweights in comparison.

But that's not how he'll begin.

He'll effectively come onto the world scene singing, "All we are saying is give peace a chance…." Swept off their feet by his power and charm and astounding abilities, the people of the world will happily join his parade.

It reminds me a little of how Rome conquered much of the world, making seemingly benevolent gestures—only later to suppress people and demand they worship Caesar or face execution. For many, the *pax Romana*, or "peace of Rome," became a terrible nightmare of persecution and violence.

It was Malcolm Muggeridge who said, "All new news is old news happening to new people."[16]

So the Antichrist will come at first with gestures of peace and brotherhood, and people will embrace him.

Antichrist and Hitler: A Comparison

Looking back in history, Adolf Hitler did much the same thing. Hitler initially rallied the support of the German people through an interesting turn of events. When Hitler emerged on the scene, Germany was in desperate financial straits. The nation was being ravaged by chaos, with many people literally starving, and Communists rioting in the streets.

When Hitler came along, he seemed to be a voice of authority in the midst of this upheaval and turmoil. He spoke to the German people about being a people of destiny, and he promised glories to come. He told them that Germany would rule the world; he said the Roman Empire would be revived, and Hitler would be its head, leading them out of their morass to unimagined heights.

His prophecies seemed to be coming true before the eyes of all as, in the next five years, he led the German economy out of shambles, built roads and schools, and managed to bring a sense of pride back to Germany again after its devastating defeat in World War I.

And after some initial reluctance, he won the churches over, too.

On one occasion he gathered many of the clergy together, assuring them that all would be well under his rule. One brave minister spoke up and said, "Well Herr Fuhrer, we know the church will be fine because Jesus said the gates of hell will not prevail against her. But our concern is for the soul of Germany."

And Hitler responded, "Oh, the soul of Germany. You just leave that to me." And they did. The rest, of course, is history.

As Hitler began to show his true colors, however, he persecuted Christians as well as Jews. Sometimes people say, "The church cooperated with Hitler." Yes, some did, not knowing what they were getting themselves into. But their eyes were undoubtedly opened when his followers went into houses of worship, removed the crosses, and put up the swastikas in their place. The fact is, many courageous believers were executed under Hitler, along with the Jewish people.

In this sense, Hitler was a prototype of the Antichrist.

In his book *Hitler's Cross*, author Erwin Lutzer writes the following about the enigma of Adolf Hitler.

> Privately Hitler prepared for war. Publicly he gave speeches about his desire for peace. Privately he enjoyed pornography. Publicly he insisted on right conduct. No swearing. No off colored jokes in his presence. At times he could be charming and forgiving. Many other times he was monstrously cruel. He prided himself on his honesty yet he reveled in his ability to deceive. The German people must be misled if the support of the masses is required, he mused. Hitler was a cauldron of contradictions. He could weep with tenderness when talking with children and rejoice over the completion of another concentration camp.[17]

That is what the Antichrist will be like. Initially he will come as a man of peace, even helping the Jews to rebuild their temple. But three and a half years into the Tribulation period, he will show his true colors. It will be at that point that the Antichrist will commit what the Bible describes as the "abomination of desolation," spoken of by Daniel the prophet, and referred to by Jesus in Matthew 24. In his second letter to the Thessalonians, Paul sets the scene like this:

> Please don't be so easily shaken and troubled by those who say that the day of the Lord has already begun ....Don't be fooled by what they say. For that day will not come until there is a great rebellion against God and the man of lawlessness is revealed—the one who brings destruction. He will exalt himself and defy every god there is and tear down every object of adoration and worship. He will position himself in the temple of God, claiming that he himself is God. (2 Thessalonians 2:2, 3-4, NLT)

The abomination takes place when the Antichrist, standing in the temple of God, commands people to worship him. War, pestilence, and famine follow in his wake as represented by the red horse, the black horse, and the pale horse that we have read about in Revelation 6.

At that time, the Antichrist will have someone called "the False Prophet" in cahoots with him, serving as his religious/spiritual leader. Revelation 19:20 says,

> But the beast was captured, and with him the false prophet who had performed the miraculous signs on his behalf. With these signs he had deluded those who had received the mark of the beast and worshiped his image. The two of them were thrown alive into the fiery lake of burning sulfur. (NIV)

The First Church of the Antichrist

Together, the beast and the false prophet will develop some kind of all-embracing religious system that will be accepted by believer and nonbeliever alike. I would imagine it to be some sort of brew of New Age mysticism with some occultism thrown in. And those who don't know any better will buy into it.

We already see this kind of thinking becoming more prevalent in our culture today as more and more people seek to make God in their own image. When push comes to shove, there really aren't that many aggressive atheists in our country; most Americans believe in God. The problem, however, is that they often believe in a god who isn't real—a god of their own making. They may borrow a little from here and a little from there and make up a few things on their own, and that becomes their belief system.

In the age of the iPod, iPhone, iMac, and now the iPad, we effectively have "iFaith" and "iGod." With iFaith and iGod, you control the home screen. You can write your own programs or apps. You can customize it to your own liking. You can leave the parts you like, such as love, forgiveness, and heaven. You can take out the parts you don't like, such as hell, judgment, and righteousness—just highlight them, and hit the "delete" key. The glaring problem with all of this is, 'iGod" is just the worship of ourselves, and that god will never save us.

That will be similar to what we see in this last days scenario that the false prophet will be promoting and the Antichrist will be pushing. It will be a mixture of old and new beliefs, shot through with occultism and it will swallow up the hearts and minds of those who are unprepared to resist.

In addition to a new one-world religion, the Antichrist will also change economics as we know them today. He will bring solutions to the global economic woes of the world through his sophisticated international ID system. The book of Revelation tells us that

> . . . he required everyone—great and small, rich and poor, slave and free—to be given a mark on the right hand or on the forehead. And no one could buy or sell anything without that mark, which was either the name of the beast or the number representing his name. Wisdom is needed to understand this. Let the one who has understanding solve the number of the beast, for it is the number of a man. His number is 666. (Revelation 13:16-18, NLT)

The New ID System

Let's consider this for a moment. We have seen the Bible predicting the collapse of the economies of the world and a new numbering system where people with some special mark can buy or sell. This would have been hard to image a hundred years ago. But not anymore. With all of our computer technology and with what is happening in the economy today, we can now see how something like this could become a reality by tomorrow morning!

One expert said,

> Amidst the global economic crisis in which upwards of 45 percent of the world's wealth has been lost in the last 18 months, talk of radically restructuring the global economic system is growing. In recent weeks leaders in Europe, Africa, and the Middle East have proposed scrapping the current economic order and going to a single common currency.[18]

Right now, the problem is that these economic planners can't decide which currency to go with. The Dollar? It has never been weaker. The

Euro? No, that's not strong, either.

A number of prominent economists are now promoting the idea of a cashless society. In fact, we're already moving rapidly in that direction, with all our technology. We have our debit cards, fast-pass MasterCards, and bar scans on almost every product. At the same time, we have developed keyless car ignitions, OnStar satellite vehicle systems, and GPS units in our little phones, iPhones, and even watches! Not to mention the fact that people have been putting microchips in dogs and cats for years now. All of this global positioning technology is handy for determining where you are and for getting to where you want to go. But it would also be handy for those who wanted to track your movements for reasons of their own.

There is even a device out now called the VeriChip—a chip that stores all of an individual's personal identification data—that some people have already had implanted in their bodies.

It makes sense, doesn't it? Who wants to pack around a massive purse or a wallet so big it can dislocate your hip? Wouldn't it be handier to have all your personal information in a tiny microchip stored just under your skin? Perhaps in the back of your hand, where you could wave it in front of a scanner?

Some people seem to think so.

Contemporary historian Arnold Toynbee wrote:

> By forcing on mankind more and more lethal weapons and at the same time making the world more and more interdependent economically, technology has brought mankind to such a degree of distress that we are ripe for the deifying of any new Caesar who might succeed in giving the world unity and peace.[19]

Yes, that's exactly right, and we can count on the fact that such a new Caesar will come. And his name will be Antichrist.

Paul-Henri Spaak, the first Secretary General of NATO, affirmed,

> We do not want another committee. We already have too many. What we want is a man of sufficient stature to hold the allegiance of all the people and lift us up out of the economic morass into which we are

sinking. Send us such a man. And whether he be a god or the devil we will receive him.[20]

Well, Mr. Spaak, he *is* going to be a devil.

He will be the Devil's son, the Antichrist. And he is coming.

This will all culminate in a final battle called the Battle of Armageddon. Out on the plains of Megiddo, the Antichrist will have ten confederated forces behind him, and he will face off with an army identified in the Bible as the Kings of the East.

But that final battle will be interrupted by the greatest event of all: the Second Coming of Jesus Christ, in all His power and glory.

Again...Where is America?

In its many prophetic passages, the Bible speaks of specific nations— and some with recognizable names. Israel is clearly identified, as is Iran (Persia) and Libya. Most likely, we can also identify Sudan, Russia, China, and perhaps even Europe. But there is no passage that one can point to that clearly would represent the reigning superpower on the face of the earth today: the United States of America.

Our absence is conspicuous. Where are we? We can only guess. But I think it is safe to say that our nation will not play a major role in the end times events. Why is that? Here are just a few possibilities.

Possibility #1 The U.S. will be decimated.

It is possible that the United States is not mentioned in Bible prophesy because our country will have been all but wiped out in a nuclear attack. We can't rule this out, because it *could* happen. I mentioned earlier that there are 27,000 nuclear weapons on the planet, and some of those weapons in the hands of rogue nations who have already threatened to use them. Would it be impossible to imagine that some terrorist group could lay hands on such weapons someday?

It's a terrible thought, and one that I hope never comes to pass.

But neither can we rule it out.

Possibility #2 The U.S. simply declines as a world power.

As we all know, nations rise and nations fall. As Mark Hitchcock pointed out in his book *Is America in Bible Prophecy?*, the might of Babylon lasted only 86 years. The powerful Persian Empire did better, hanging around for 208 years. The glory of Greece was eclipsed after 268 years. Mighty Rome lasted for eight centuries. The British Empire endured for almost 250 years. And now, as of this writing, the United States of America is 233 years old and counting.

Every nation's days are numbered. And as our dollar gets weaker and the Euro and other currencies get stronger, as China and others nations become economic powerhouses, you see how this could happen. We could just simply diminish as a world power. To use the terminology of the poet T. S. Eliot, America might end, "not with a bang, but a whimper."[21]

Possibility #3 Many in America will be raptured.

This is my favorite option by far! America may not be mentioned in Bible prophesy because a great revival sweeps our nation, and millions become believers in Jesus Christ.

How would that remove us from the world stage?

If the Lord graciously sent a spiritual awakening to our country so that many came to faith in Christ, the rapture of the church would radically change our nation overnight.

If you polled Americans today—all 308 million of them—approximately half of them would claim to be "born again." So at least 150 million Americans would say right now, "I am a Christian." Are they? God only knows, but I tend to doubt that. So let's cut that number in half. What if there were 75 million Christians in our country? Let's make it even smaller. Let's say for the sake of a point that 50 million of us are genuine followers of Jesus.

Can you imagine what would happen if 50 million Americans suddenly disappeared? Can you begin to calculate the effect that would have on industry, government, the military, business, agriculture, education, and medicine? It could cut us down overnight.

After a scenario like that, it's easy to imagine how the Antichrist could emerge on the scene with a calm voice and an aura of great competence and authority, bringing startling economic solutions to the world's woes, and a strong global world view. The America left after the rapture of the church might easily fall in line and become just another one of the nations confederated behind him.

How Should We Respond?

So what are we supposed to do in light of all this? I think that we as the church ought to do what we do best: We need to pray for our country like never before. And we need to reach out to a lost world with the gospel like never before.

The answer for America's problems is not a military one, but a spiritual one. We need more people hearing about who Jesus is and what He promises, not some vague, inclusive, whatever-you-believe-god-to-be spirituality.

We need to get back to the true God of the Bible. The God of Abraham, Isaac, and Jacob. The God who sent His Son Jesus Christ to be born in the manger, to die on the cross, and to rise again from the dead three days later. If we turn to back to God—to *that* God—He promises He will bless us.

Have we been doing that as a nation?

No, we haven't. In fact, we've been drifting further and further from Him. It seems like every time you turn around a new law is being passed to restrict the practice of one's faith, and it seems like those laws are always aimed against Christians. America seemingly will tolerate anything and anyone as long as he or she isn't proclaiming Christ or that the Bible is the Word of God.

But here is the promise of God in Scripture to any nation, including ours. In 2 Chronicles 7:14, God says, "If My people which are called by My name will humble themselves, and pray and seek My face, and turn from their wicked ways, then, I will hear from heaven, and will forgive their sin and heal their land."

I want you to notice where God directs His remarks. He doesn't say, "If Congress will turn from its wicked ways." (Though it should.) He didn't say, "If Hollywood would turn from its wicked ways." (Though it ought to.) Or, "If the President would turn from his wicked ways."

No, God doesn't point His finger at the White House. He points His finger at *God's* house. He points His finger at you and me. He says, "If *My people, which are called by My name…*"

It's so easy for us to say, "If only those Democrats would change," or "If only those Republicans would see the light." Or maybe, "If only the mainstream media would get its act together." No doubt there are plenty of problems to go around in a nation such as ours.

But God is speaking to His own people in this passage.

He says, My people need to live as they ought to live. My people need to humble themselves and pray. My people need to turn from evil habits and preoccupations and distractions. And if that happens, God says that He will hear from heaven, forgive our sins, and heal our land.

That, my friend, is called revival.

And it's the best hope this nation—or any other nation—has for protection and prosperity in turbulent times such as these.

It may indeed by America's only hope.

Chapter Four

ISRAEL, MAGOG, AND THE RAPTURE

"But when you see Jerusalem surrounded by armed forces, Then you will know that the time of her devastation has arrived." —Luke 21:20, PHILLIPS

When I first became a Christian back in 1970, lots of people were talking about the return of Jesus Christ. The top selling book of that entire decade was the *Late Great Planet Earth*, by Hal Lindsey, which spoke in depth about Bible prophecy and the signs of the times.

Driving around the roads and freeways, you would see bumper stickers with slogans like "Maranatha," and, "Jesus is coming," and "In case of rapture this car will be left unmanned," or maybe, "Get right or get left."

There was a sense of expectancy among so many of us that we could be the generation that would see the return of the Lord.

Well, that was forty years ago, and I've gone through quite a few "Jesus is coming" bumper stickers since those days.

Was my hope displaced?

Did I get it wrong?

Did we misread the signs of the times?

Not at all. God is not late, and the Lord will return to this earth at the appointed hour that has been predetermined in the councils of eternity. But there may be a reason why Jesus didn't come when we were hoping He would in 1970.

Consider this: Millions and millions of men and women, boys and girls have come to Jesus since 1970.

The Bible reminds us: "The Lord isn't really being slow about his promise to return, as some people think. No, he is being patient for your sake. He does not want anyone to perish, so he is giving more time for everyone to repent" (2 Peter 3:9, NLT).

It's all in the Lord's hands, of course, but I do believe that somewhere on this planet there is a particular man or a woman whom the Lord is waiting for, and when that person finally places faith in Jesus Christ, we will be caught up to meet the Lord in the air, in what we call the Rapture of the Church.

Why do I believe this? Because all around me there are signs of the times. We've already considered one of the "super signs" of the last days, which was the re-gathering of the nation Israel in their ancient homeland.

That was against all odds. It was something that had no precedent in human history that a nation and a people that had been scattered throughout the four corners of the earth would gather again where they had once been and form a nation.

Jesus said that this generation that sees this happen will not pass away until all these things will be fulfilled.[22] Once the Jewish people had returned to their homeland and became a nation on May 14, 1948, you might say that the prophetic clock started to tick. It is a very important date in Bible prophecy.

But the Bible not only said that the Lord would gather the Jews back to their homeland again, it said that Jerusalem would end up being a source of conflict in the end times. What's interesting to me is that on May 14, 1948, Israel did not possess all of Jerusalem. In fact, that didn't happen until the 1967 War, when Israeli forces captured the old city and reunified all of Jerusalem, so the city was under Jewish control for the first time in centuries.

That, of course, is where the rub comes in. Jerusalem remains at the heart of the Israeli-Palestinian conflict, with many Arab leaders worldwide insisting that Jerusalem and the entire West Bank are rightly Palestinian territory, and must ultimately be given back as a condition of peace.

But here's the problem with that. God gave Israel and the city of Jerusalem to the Jewish people. He made that promise to them, and they're not going to give it up again. Nor should they.

Checking the Checklist

The Bible is the one book that dares to predict the future. Not once, not twice, but hundreds of times. We can look back now and see that many of those prophecies have already been fulfilled. But not all of them! Some remain to be fulfilled, and we may be the generation where that begins to take place.

It's not a big stretch for God to predict the future. God can speak to future things as easily as you and I might discuss the past or present. In fact, God can predict the future far more accurately than you and I can recall the past.

I guess you might say I have a few issues with forgetting things.

My wife seems to remember every detail of everything. I will come home and describe something that happened to me, and she catches every detail. Then, a couple days later, I will be re-describing the events to someone else and my wife will say, "No, Greg. You've got it wrong. Here's what happened."

I will look at her say, "You weren't even there!"

"I know," she'll reply. "But I was there when you told this story the first time, and now you're leaving out some of the details.

Amazing.

As much as I may struggle to remember things with any degree of accuracy, however, God has perfect retention (if want to call it that). In fact, He sees the past, present, and future *simultaneously*.

Tomorrow is like yesterday to God. Every day is before Him with equal clarity. The Lord does not forget things, nor does He learn new things.

He literally knows everything—past, present and future.

So let's just take out our checklist of events and see what has already transpired.

The Bible says Israel will be scattered to the four corners of the earth. Did that happen? Yes. *Check*.

Israel will be re-gathered as a nation. Did that happen? Yes. *Check*.

Israel will regain the city of Jerusalem. Has that happened? Yes. *Check*.

Israel will be isolated from the other nations of the world. Is this happening? Yes. *Check*.

Israel will be attacked by a nation to her north, bent on her destruction. Has that happened? Not yet. But we could easily envision such a scenario.

Jerusalem will be at the center of the conflicts of the world. Not Rome. Not Paris. Not London. Not New York City, but the ancient, tiny little city of Jerusalem. We read in Luke 21:20 (NLT): "And when you see Jerusalem surrounded by armies, then you will know that the time of its destruction has arrived."

In Zechariah 12:2-3 (NLT) God says, "I will make Jerusalem and Judah like an intoxicating drink to all the nearby nations that send their armies to besiege Jerusalem. On that day I will make Jerusalem a heavy stone, a burden for the world. None of the nations who try to lift it will escape unscathed."

John Walvoord, a respected expert on Bible prophecy, made this statement:

The prophecies about Jerusalem make it clear that the holy city will be in the center of the world events in the end time. The conflict between Israel and the Palestinian Arabs will focus more and more attention on Jerusalem. In all of the situations Jerusalem is the city to watch as the city of prophetic destiny prepares to act out her final role.[23]

Israel is so tiny! At one point the nation is only nine miles wide. Yet God says she will be at the center of the end time events. And it is happening just as the Bible promised it would.

"Them Bones"

There is a startling passage in the book of Ezekiel, written almost 600 years before Jesus was born, that speaks to Israel's reemergence as a nation.

> The LORD took hold of me, and I was carried away by the Spirit of the LORD to a valley filled with bones. He led me around among the old, dry bones that covered the valley floor. They were scattered everywhere across the ground. Then he asked me, "Son of man, can these bones become living people again?"
>
> "O Sovereign LORD," I replied, "you alone know the answer to that."
>
> Then he said to me, "Speak to these bones and say, 'Dry bones, listen to the word of the Lord! This is what the Sovereign LORD says: Look! I am going to breathe into you and make you live again! I will put flesh and muscles on you and cover you with skin. I will put breath into you, and you will come to life. Then you will know that I am the LORD.'" (Ezekiel 37: 1-6, NLT)

Now I have preached to some dead audiences before, but nothing like this! God says to Ezekiel, "Preach a sermon to the dry bones." Why would he want to do that?

Because God said they were going to live again.

The Lord gives us the interpretation of what the prophet says in verses 11 to 14 of Ezekiel 37.

> Then he said to me, "Son of man, these bones represent the people of Israel. They are saying, 'We have become old, dry bones—all hope is gone.' Now give them this message from the Sovereign LORD: O my people, I will open your graves of exile and cause you to rise again. Then I will bring you back to the land of Israel. When this happens, O my people, you will know that I am the LORD. I will put my Spirit in you, and you will live and return home to your own land. Then you will know that I am the LORD. You will see that I have done everything just as I promised. I, the LORD, have spoken!" (NLT)

It's a picture of the re-gathered nation of Israel in her own land, and it has happened just as God said it would.

In 2010, Israeli Prime Minister Benjamin Netanyahu was speaking in Poland, commemorating the 65th anNIversary of liberation of

Auschwitz. Speaking on the actual site of the Nazi death camp, the Prime Minister said these words:

> After the Holocaust, the Jewish people rose from ashes and destruction, from a terrible pain that can never be healed. Armed with the Jewish spirit, the justice of man, and the vision of the prophets, we sprouted new branches and grew deep roots. Dry bones became covered with flesh, a spirit filled them, and they lived and stood on their own feet. As Ezekiel prophesied: "Then He said unto me: These bones are the whole House of Israel. They say, 'Our bones are dried up, our hope is gone; we are doomed.' Prophecy, therefore, and say to them: Thus said the Lord God: I am going to open your graves and lift you out of your graves, O My people, and bring you to the land of Israel."

> I stand here today on the ground where so many of my people perished—and I am not alone. The State of Israel and all the Jewish people stand with me. We bow our heads to honor your memory and lift our heads as we raise our flag—a flag of blue and white with a Star of David in its center. And everyone sees. And everyone hears. And everyone knows—that our hope is not lost.[24]

It's one thing when a pastor makes a statement like this, but when the Prime Minister of Israel says it, it's breathtaking! I wonder if Mr. Netanyahu also looks for clues about Israel's future from Ezekiel 38-39.

If he does, then he can hardly fail to notice that in Ezekiel 38, the Lord speaks of a large and powerful nation to the north of the newly established Jewish homeland, along with a number of her allies, invading Israel. This has not yet happened. So let's see what it says.

> This is another message that came to me from the LORD: "Son of man, prophesy against Gog of the land of Magog, the prince who rules over the nations of Meshech and Tubal. Give him this message from the Sovereign LORD: Gog, I am your enemy! I will turn you around and put hooks into your jaws to lead you out to your destruction. I will mobilize your troops and cavalry and make you a vast and mighty horde, all fully armed. Persia, Ethiopia, and Libya will join you, too, with all their weapons." (Ezekiel 38:1-5, NLT)

Drop down to verses 8-11:

> Get ready; be prepared! Keep all the armies around you mobilized, and take command of them. A long time from now you will be called

into action. In the distant future you will swoop down on the land of Israel, which will be lying in peace after her recovery from war and after the return of her people from many lands. You and all your allies—a vast and awesome horde—will roll down on them like a storm and cover the land like a cloud.

This is what the Sovereign LORD says: At that time evil thoughts will come to your mind, and you will devise a wicked scheme. You will say, 'Israel is an unprotected land filled with unwalled villages! I will march against her and destroy these people who live in such confidence!' (NLT)

Magog?

Now who could that possibly be? And who are these allies that march with her? It is believed by many that Magog is speaking of modern day Russia. Why is this believed?

The reasoning goes like this: Magog was the second son of Noah's son Japheth who, according to the ancient historian Josephus, settled north of the Black Sea. Tubal and Meshech, also mentioned here in Ezekiel 38, were the fifth and sixth sons of Japheth whose descendents settled south of the Black Sea.

These tribes intermarried and became known as Magog. They settled to the north of Israel. In Ezekiel 39:2 (NLT) God says to them, "I will turn you around and drive you toward the mountains of Israel, bringing you from the distant north."

So all Bible directions are given in relation to Israel. And if you look to the extreme north of Israel today you will find the mighty nation of Russia.

Now here is where it really gets interesting. Look at the allies that march with Russia. We have Ethiopia (that would be modern day Sudan), Libya, and Persia, which is modern day Iran. These are all Islamic cultures, and they are all anti-Israel. Russia has five arms deals in play right now with Libya alone. And Persia? It wasn't until March 21, 1935 that Persia changed her name to what we now call Iran, a recent ally of Russia.

So here is the alliance that God says will form against Israel, and there's really nothing about it that surprises us. It's already taking shape before our eyes.

The Rise of Iran/Persia

Did you know that Russia recently signed a billion dollar deal to sell missiles and other weapons to Iran? There are over 1,000 Iranian nuclear scientists who have been trained in Russia by Russian scientists. A recent news article quotes the Russian deputy foreign minister as saying, "Russia is determined to boost its military technical ties with Iran."[25]

It may be in today's headline, but it was all prophesied in the Bible, thousands of years ago.

The current president of Iran, Mahmoud Ahmadinejad, is a disciple of the Ayatollah Khomeini. Khomeini was the one who launched the successful 1979 revolution, driving out the Shah of Iran and turning Iran into a strict Moslem state. And in 2005 Ahmadinejad was called before the U.N. Security Council to explain his continued determination to develop nuclear weapons.

He began his speech by declaring, "In the name of the god of mercy, compassion, peace, freedom, and justice...." He ended his speech with a prayer to Allah, and I want you to note his words very carefully. "I pray," he says, speaking to Allah, "For you to hasten the emergence of your last repository, the promised one, the pure and perfect human being, the one who will fill this world with justice and peace."[26]

Of whom was Ahmadinejad speaking? In this particular branch of Islam, "the promised one" refers to the "Twelfth Imam"—an Islamic messiah. And it is believed that this messiah cannot appear until there is a period of great chaos. So Ahmadinejad feels that by stirring up trouble threatening Israel and even the United States, his nation can bring about the chaos that would bring this Twelfth Iman, this Islamic messiah, onto the scene.

Just recently a top official with Iran's revolutionary force warned that Iran will blow up the heart of Israel if the United States or the Jewish state attacks it first. He said, "Should a single American or

Zionist missile land in our country, before the dust settles Iranian missiles will blow up the heart of Israel."[27]

No. Actually they won't.

That's not the way events will play out. It will play out in the way that God has said it will.

I recently had the opportunity to attend a briefing by a top ranking general with the Israeli military, and a close confidant of President Benjamin Netanyahu.

How does Israel view these threats from Iran?

"We take these very threats very seriously," he said. "We don't think they are empty threats. And we will respond appropriately."[28]

Israel is saying in so many words they will do what needs to be done, with or without the help of the United States, to stop this threat.

Could this explode and culminate in the scenario we read about in Ezekiel 38 and 39?

Yes it could.

Will it?

That I don't know. Perhaps and perhaps not. We have to be very careful in interpreting the headlines today. But here is what we do know: A large force from the north, identified as Magog, will attack Israel. It will happen, but we don't know why or when at this point. There are many things taking place in our world however that make me realize that it could happen at any time.

And quickly.

When these events begin, they will occur in rapid succession, like falling dominoes.

But What Does This Mean to Me?

Consider this: When Magog and her allies attack Israel, God will intervene and decimate her army and the armies of the allies as well. And because of this, the Jewish people will give glory to God.

When you go to Israel today, you might be surprised to learn that most Israelis are not believers in God. Many of them are atheistic.

Certainly you will find very few Jewish people that believe in Jesus as their Messiah. There are some, thank God, but not all that many.

But when the Holy Spirit is poured out upon Israel after He drives back the invading armies of Magog, there will be a revival in Israel and many, many, many Jewish people will come to believe *Yeshua Hamashiach*. Jesus is the Messiah.

This outpouring of the Spirit on Israel, however, can't happen until the full gathering of the Gentiles is accomplished. What does that mean? Most people who read these pages are Gentiles, not Jewish by birth. As Paul explains in Romans 11, we have been effectively grafted into the promises God originally offered to Israel. This is the time when God is working with the non-Jews, the Gentiles. But this time will come to a close, and then the Spirit will be poured out again on the land and people of Israel. But before that can happen, God needs to wrap things up with us.

In Romans 11:25 (NLT), Paul says, "I want you to understand this mystery, dear brothers and sisters, so that you will not feel proud and start bragging. Some of the Jews have hard hearts, but this will last only until the complete number of Gentiles comes to Christ."

The complete number of Gentiles.

In other words, as I said earlier, until the last Gentile person finally believes in Jesus. And then…we will be gone. Caught up. Raptured. In a microsecond. And we will meet the Lord in the air, and be with Him forever.

So that means when we see these events in the world beginning to happen, we need to look up, for our redemption is drawing near.

"I Will Receive You…"

When we speak of the rapture of the church, there are some who will say, "The word 'rapture' isn't even in the Bible."

Maybe not, but the event certainly is!

For the Lord Himself will descend from heaven with a shout, with the voice of an archangel, and with the trumpet of God. And the

dead in Christ will rise first. Then we who are alive and remain shall be caught up together with them in the clouds to meet the Lord in the air. And thus we shall always be with the Lord.
(1 Thessalonians 4:16-17)

Over in John 14:2-3, Jesus said,

In My Father's house are many mansions; if it were not so, I would have told you. I go to prepare a place for you. And if I go and prepare a place for you, I will come again and receive you to Myself; that where I am, there you may be also.

That phrase "receive you" means to take you by force.

And then over in Matthew 24:40-42, Jesus says, "Two men will be in the field: one will be taken and the other left. Two women will be grinding at the mill: one will be taken and the other left. Watch therefore, for you do not know what hour your Lord is coming."

John addressed it as well in 1 John 3:2 (NLT), "Yes, dear friends, we are already God's children, and we can't even imagine what we will be like when Christ returns. But we do know that when he comes we will be like him, for we will see him as he really is."

Paul speaks of this same event in 1 Corinthians 15:51–52:

Behold, I tell you a mystery: We shall not all sleep, but we shall all be changed—in a moment, in the twinkling of an eye, at the last trumpet. For the trumpet will sound, and the dead will be raised incorruptible, and we shall be changed.

Now imagine this for a moment. In an instant, all over the world, millions of believers are caught up to meet the Lord in the air.

When Paul made his statement about the rapture to the believers of Thessalonica, there was some concern about their loved ones who had already gone on to heaven. Death was a far more common occurrence to first century believers than perhaps it is to us today, at least in the United States. These people lived with the threat of imminent death of their friends and loved ones who were believers in Jesus. Why? Because the church was persecuted, and thousands upon thousands of believers were martyred.

These believers in Thessalonica were left wondering, "What does it all mean? How does this work with our loved ones who are no longer with us?" So Paul gives them these words:

> But I do not want you to be ignorant, brethren, concerning those who have fallen asleep, lest you sorrow as others who have no hope. For if we believe that Jesus died and rose again, even so God will bring with Him those who sleep in Jesus.

> For this we say to you by the word of the Lord, that we who are alive and remain until the coming of the Lord will by no means precede those who are asleep. (1 Thessalonians 4:13-15)

It's interesting that the Bible doesn't speak of believers as being dead; it speaks of them as being asleep. No, the Bible is not in denial. It simply chooses a different word. You see, when you are a believer in Jesus, you never die. Jesus said, "I am the resurrection and the life. He who believes in Me, though he may die, he shall live. And whoever lives and believes in Me shall never die. Do you believe this?" (John 11:25).

So death for the believer is compared to sleep. It's funny how you dread sleep so much when you're young, and look forward to it when you're old. Our four-year-old granddaughter has to take a nap every day, and she doesn't like it one bit. She fights it.

But Stella's grandpa looks forward to his naps—even if it's only a ten minute catnap where I put my feet up on my desk and slip into dreamland. Just a few minutes of sleep and I wake up refreshed.

Really, a nap is a beautiful picture, and speaks of someone who is at peace.

The Bible here isn't suggesting that when a believer dies he or she goes into some kind of "soul sleep." It is rather a picture used to describe a person who is at peace. The reality is that people in heaven are active, worshiping, and serving the Lord.

So Paul is saying, "Listen. I don't want you guys to worry about this. Those who have fallen asleep, those who have gone before you, you're going to see them again. There will be a great reunion, and you'll all be together again."

Perhaps you're recently lost a loved one to death, and you're enduring a time of grief right now. Paul writes this passage in Thessalonians just for you. Remember this, he is saying. You could be going about your business one day, thinking about your departed loved one, and then suddenly, so quickly that it can't be measured with time, you will be seeing that person face to face. Mothers and fathers will be reunited with sons and daughters. Husbands will be reunited with wives and wives with husbands. Children with their parents. Brothers with brothers. Sisters with sisters. Friends with friends. Your sorrow will immediately vanish and be replaced by ecstatic joy.

But not only will you find yourself reunited with loved ones, you will open your eyes in the very presence of Love Himself, the Lord Jesus Christ. That is what will happen in the rapture.

I personally look forward to this so much, as our oldest son Christopher went to be with the Lord in July of 2008.

We grieve his loss deeply each and every day.

We miss him so very, very much.

We long to see him and speak with him.

That day is coming for us, and all of us who have had loved ones precede us to heaven.

So think about that, and let heaven fill your thoughts. What if it happened today? Is that escapism? If it is, then count me in. I'll accept that label. The rapture will be a great escape, and I don't mind admitting that I'm looking forward to it.

C. S. Lewis said, "A continual looking forward to the eternal world is not a form of escapism or wishful thinking, but one of the things a Christian is meant to do."[29]

To summarize, let's just briefly consider some of the effects the rapture will have on each of us.

#1 The rapture means no death.

There is a generation that will not see death. They will go straight into the presence of God. Will we be that generation? Very possibly. We need to be ready.

#2 The rapture is instantaneous.

First Corinthians 15:51-52 says, "Behold, I tell you a mystery: We shall not all sleep, but we shall all be changed— in a moment, in the twinkling of an eye…"

It has been said that the twinkling of an eye is about 1/1000 of a second. How fast is a second? And this is a thousandth of that? If we have the privilege of being raptured, there will no real sense of departure and arrival, we will simply *be there*, in the Lord's presence.

#3 The rapture is a transformation.

In that moment, God will give you a brand new resurrection body. Perhaps you struggle now with the effects of old age, disease or some other physical difficulty or problem. All of that will be gone in an instant. Age melts away. Disability disappears. Sorrows are replaced by pure joy.

Philippians 3:20 gives us these glorious words:

> But we are citizens of heaven, where the Lord Jesus Christ lives. And we are eagerly waiting for him to return as our Savior. He will take these weak mortal bodies of ours and change them into glorious bodies like his own, using the same mighty power that he will use to conquer everything, everywhere. (NLT)

$4 The rapture will be a rescue operation.

In 1 Thessalonians 1:10 (NIV), Paul declares: "They tell how you turned to God from idols to serve the living and true God, and to wait for his Son from heaven, whom he raised from the dead—Jesus, who rescues us from the coming wrath."

From what is He rescuing us? The wrath to come. What is that a reference to? The tribulation period, inaugurated by the emergence of the Antichrist, and lasting for seven years. So God is sending his special ops team of Michael and His angels to evacuate the church— to get us out of here before the tribulation begins.

Sometimes there is confusion about the Second Coming and the rapture. Some people think it is one event. But the Bible is very clear it is speaking of two distinct events.

The rapture will be a stealth event; the Second Coming a very public one.

In the rapture we meet the Lord in the air; in the Second Coming, He returns to the earth.

In the rapture He comes *for* His church; in the Second Coming, He returns *with* His church.

In the rapture He comes before judgment; in the Second Coming, He comes with judgment.

So how should this affect us today? How should I respond to these truths? Very simply, I need to walk with God.

Walk with God

We have a great Old Testament prototype of these things in the life of a man named Enoch. Enoch had what we might describe as a solo rapture.

In Genesis 5:24 we read these intriguing words: "And Enoch walked with God and was not, for God took him." That phrase "God took him" could be rendered "God *translated* him." In other words, God carried him over or carried him across. Enoch didn't have to die like everybody else. He just took a walk one day and didn't come home. Or maybe I should say he took a walk and went home! He started on one shore and ended up on another.

He walked with God.

Are you walking with God? Notice it doesn't say, "Enoch sprinted with God." He *walked* with God.

I was always pretty good as a short distance sprinter, but never much good as a long distance runner. I would have this great, explosive burst of energy, but then I would quickly give out.

A number of years ago I did a bicycle trip with a bunch of people who ride all the time. So there I was on a nice road bike, full of vim and vigor, zooming by people, and feeling pretty good about myself. But then about halfway through the ride, all of that energy started to evaporate. By the time the trip was over, one of the guys had to push me on my bike, because old Greg had run out of steam.

Many people are like that spiritually. They have a burst of energy and say, "I love the Lord so much. I'm really going to follow Him." But all too soon, they crash and burn. Then they get up again and they go for awhile—only to crash and burn again.

Here's the thing: Just walk with God.

Don't be in a big hurry. Be regular, be consistent, and stay at it. Be disciplined enough to maintain that relationship. Walking implies steady effort, and speaks of regularity—doing something over and over.

Remember when your kids first learned to walk? I remember when our granddaughter Stella took her first steps. I was over at Christopher and his wife Brittany's house, and they were talking in the kitchen with my wife, Cathe, while I was playing in the other room with Stella. She was standing up, hanging onto a chair or the couch or something, and she put out one foot and took a step.

"That looked like a step to me," I said.

Then she did another, and I was getting excited. "That's a second step!" Then she did a third, and fell down. I yelled from the living room, "Stella just walked!"

They came running in. "No, not really!"

"Yes," I said triumphantly. "And I saw it first!" Then she did it again for all of us, and that made it an exciting day.

We're like that as we start out in our relationship with Christ. We take our first steps, and then we trip and we fall and hit our head on the table. Get up again. Fall down again. Get up again…and gradually gain balance and get strong. Kids learning to walk never give up, and neither should we.

That's walking with God. You just stay with it, day by day, hour by hour, step by step, and seek to be consistent in your relationship with Jesus Christ.

"As you therefore have received Christ Jesus the Lord, so walk in Him" *(Colossians 2:6).*

"Walk in the Spirit, and you shall not fulfill the lust of the flesh"
(Galatians 5:16).

"Walk in love, as Christ also has loved us and given Himself for us"
(Ephesians 5:2).

"If we walk in the light as He is in the light, we have fellowship with one another, and the blood of Jesus Christ His Son cleanses us from all sin"
(1 John 1:7).

Jesus Christ is coming back, and it could happen at any time. This year. This month. This week. Today.

And when He comes, I want Him to find me walking with Him. Isn't that a great thought? You could take one step on earth, and then find that your next step is into His presence.

Come soon, Lord. Come soon.

Chapter Five
THE SECOND COMING OF JESUS CHRIST

*"The One you are looking for will come suddenly to his Temple— the Messenger
of God's promises, to bring you great joy. Yes, he is surely coming," says the Lord
Almighty. "But who can live when he appears? Who can endure his coming?
For he is like a blazing fire refining precious metal...." —Malachi 3:1-2, TLB*

N ewspapers have a certain kind of headline type that they
reserve only for mega events.

They call it, "Second Coming type."

It's the kind of type that was used when Pearl Harbor was attacked,
when President Kennedy was assassinated in Dallas, and when the
terrorists attacked the World Trade Center. It's the kind of type that
leaps off the page and says *read me.*

Why do they call it "Second Coming type"? I think it's an implicit
recognition that the greatest news event of human history will be the
Second Coming of Jesus Christ.

Did you know that many people believe Christ is coming back?
It's true—and even among people who don't claim to be Christians.
A Gallup poll found that 66 percent of Americans believe Jesus Christ
is coming back to this earth sometime in the near future. And by the
way, that was 25 percent *more* than those who claim to be born again.[30]

As they look at the way the world is going, there is a sense even
among nonbelievers that Christ will come back again to set things right.
The Bible speaks of this event frequently. In fact, one verse out of every
twenty-five makes some mention of the Lord's return. Jesus Himself

talked about it in what we call the Olivet Discourse in Matthew 24:

> Immediately after the distress of those days
> 'the sun will be darkened,
> and the moon will not give its light;
> the stars will fall from the sky,
> and the heavenly bodies will be shaken.'

> At that time the sign of the Son of Man will appear in the sky, and all the nations of the earth will mourn. They will see the Son of Man coming on the clouds of the sky, with power and great glory. (vv. 29-30, NIV)

Everyone who has put his or her faith in Christ will have the privilege of being there on that greatest of days.

Before Christ returns to the earth, however, another event must first transpire.

Armageddon

That very word sounds ominous, threatening, and very final. It's true—Armageddon will be the final conflict of mankind.

Many today invoke the term when seeking to make a point. Dr. David Jeremiah tells the story of General Douglas MacArthur, standing on the deck of the USS Missouri in Tokyo Harbor, when he was signing a peace agreement with the Japanese, effectively bringing World War II to a close. The general made this statement: "We have had our last chance. If we do not now devise some greater and more equitable system, Armageddon will be at our door."[31]

Soon after taking office as the fortieth President of the United States, Ronald Reagan was astounded by the complexities of the Middle East. On Friday, May 15, 1981, President Reagan wrote these words in his diary: "Sometimes I wonder if we are destined to witness Armageddon."[32]

Three weeks later on Sunday, June 7, President Reagan heard that Israel had bombed the Iraqi nuclear reactor. And later in that day he wrote again in his diary: "I swear I believe Armageddon is near."[33]

I wonder what General MacArthur and President Reagan would

think of events that have happened in recent days in our country. The destruction of the World Trade Center and the attack on the Pentagon by Islamic terrorists…the arming of Iraq and of North Korea with nuclear weapons…the repeated threats by Iran to use nuclear weapons to wipe Israel off the face of the map.

Yes, we are going to face Armageddon.

But understand that Armageddon is not simply one final battle. The word Armageddon comes from a word that means Valley of Megiddo. But really when we talk about Armageddon we are talking about the final conflict in this valley.

That valley lies within the borders of Israel today, and you can go and visit it. I've been there numerous times on our tours of the Holy Land. Many battles have already been fought in this vast plain. Deborah and Barak defeated the Canaanites there, and Gideon defeated the Midianites. We know that King Saul was killed by the Philistines on this battlefield of Megiddo.

Why should this particular valley be the scene for the final battle of mankind? Napoleon himself gave an answer to that. In 1799, Napoleon stood at Megiddo and said, "All the armies of the world could maneuver their forces on this vast plain. There is no place in the world more suited for war than this. It is the most natural battleground on the whole earth."[34]

The Kings of the East

After World War I ended, it was hoped that it would be "the war to end all wars," because 10 million people lost their lives in that horrific conflict. But it took only 20 years for an even more terrible war to break out across our planet. In World War II, 50 million people died around the world.

It would be nice to say that we could reach the place in our world where there would be no more war.

But friends, war is still going to happen.

Jesus said so.

He told us that one of the signs of the end times would be wars and rumors of wars which will eventually culminate in the great battle of Armageddon.

As far as we can see in Scripture (and as I've mentioned), the United States of America doesn't seem to be a major player in that final conflict.

In fact the major players of the end times events will be the Antichrist, the ten nations confederated under him, and the kings of the east. These are the opposing forces that will come together in the valley of Megiddo, for humanity's last war, as described in Revelation 16:14:

> For they are spirits of demons, performing signs, which go out to the kings of the earth and of the whole world, to gather them to the battle of that great day of God Almighty.

Who are the kings of the east? We're given a clue in Revelation 9:16, where we're told that they can field an army of 200 million men. Who on earth could field an army that large? Really only one nation qualifies, and that would be China. Are the "kings of the east" China? No one can say with complete certainty, but there are some interesting reasons why we might think that is a possibility.

Not long ago, *Newsweek* featured a cover story called "China Century," where the writers made the case that "the future belongs to China."

The article says of China: "It is already the world's fastest-growing large economy, and the second largest holder of foreign-exchange reserves, mainly dollars. It has the world's largest army (2.5 million men) and the fourth largest defense budget, which is rising by more than 10 percent annually. Whether or not it overtakes the United States economically, which looks to me like a distant prospect, it is the powerful new force on the global scene."[35]

The *Newsweek* writers go on to say: "For centuries, the rest of the world was a stage for the ambitions and interests of the West's great powers, but China's rise, along with that of India and the continuing weight of Japan, represent the third shift in global power—the rise of Asia."[36]

China is currently the largest nation on the face of the earth, with a population of 1 billion 300 million people. The rapid buildup of their military has caused our own military experts great concern in recent days.

In 1997 China announced that they could raise an army of 352 million soldiers. That means that they could send 200 million to invade the Middle East, and still have 152 million soldiers to defend their homeland.

Here's what I find so interesting: When John wrote these words about the kings of the east coming through the dried up river Euphrates and marching on the valley of Megiddo, there weren't even 200 million people on the face of the earth. But today, this prophecy could happen before our very eyes.

We don't know with certainty who the kings of the east are, but this much we know: This massive army meets up with the forces of the Antichrist in mankind's final conflagration.

Bright Lights in Deepest Darkness

The Great Tribulation will be an intensely dark time in our world, when wickedness will reign freely. After he shows his true colors, the Antichrist will begin to hunt down and martyr Jewish people as well as Christians. Bottom line: if you don't have the mark of the beast on your body, you are put to death.

Despite this dark backdrop and bleak scenario, however, God will still get His Word out. In fact, the world will experience one of the greatest revivals in human history happen during the tribulation period.

We as Christians won't be there for it. We will be in heaven at this point, because the rapture will happen before the tribulation begins. But God's Word assures us that He will do a great work, even in earth's deepest hour of darkness.

Sometimes, people will ask me, "Won't the Holy Spirit be out of the world at this point? Isn't He going to be removed?"

The Bible doesn't say that, but here is what it does say:

For the mystery of lawlessness is already at work; only He who now restrains will do so until He is taken out of the way. And then the lawless one will be revealed, whom the Lord will consume with the breath of His mouth and destroy with the brightness of His coming. (2 Thessalonians 2:7-8)

Yes, once we have completed our work on earth and we are caught up to meet Him in heaven, wickedness will indeed break loose. But that doesn't mean the Holy Spirit will be removed. It just means that *the Church* will be removed. Otherwise, how could people come to Christ without the work of the Holy Spirit? They couldn't. And the Holy Spirit will not be removed.

The Lord will be raising up His faithful witnesses during the tribulation. First of all, many people will come to faith after the rapture. They'll show up for church on a Sunday, and (hopefully) it will be empty. Many will say to themselves, "It was all true." They'll try to call their Christian friends on their cell phones, and there won't be any answer. At that point, they will realize what has taken place and that they have been left behind to face the tribulation period. I have no doubt that many will come to faith at that time, responding to the Holy Spirit the same as they would now.

The Bible also tells us that God will raise up 144,000 Jews who will receive Jesus as their Messiah. This vast group of evangelists will have divine protection on them as they travel around the world preaching the gospel—like 144,000 kosher Billy Grahams! And they will do a great job in reaching many.

If those things weren't enough, there will also be what we might describe as an angelic mop-up operation taking place as well. Sometimes people will say, "Christ can't come back until the gospel is preached to the whole world." And they base that on the statement of Jesus when He says in Matthew 24:14, "And this gospel of the kingdom will be preached in all the world for a witness to the nations, then will the end come."

That statement, however, isn't making reference to something that must happen before the rapture, but rather must happen before the Second Coming. So here's my point: Even if the 144,000 and others miss evangelizing certain people, there will still be one final opportunity. Looking through the years into the future, the apostle John saw an amazing sight:

> Then I saw another angel flying in the midst of heaven, having the everlasting gospel to preach to those who dwell on the earth—to every nation, tribe, tongue, and people—saying with a loud voice, "Fear God and give glory to Him, for the hour of His judgment has come; and worship Him who made heaven and earth, the sea and springs of water." (Revelation 14:6-7)

Perhaps the most intriguing witnesses that God will raise up in the tribulation period, however, will be the two witnesses. These are two men whom God will put in place, who will have a powerful impact on people during those stressful days. They will have a powerful miracle ministry, including the ability to call fire down from heaven and also to stop the rain and turn water to blood. Who will these two witnesses be?

I would suggest they will probably be Moses and Elijah. You'll remember from the book of Exodus that Moses was given the ability to turn water into blood, and in 1 Kings God enabled Elijah to call down fire from heaven.

Also it was Moses and Elijah who appeared with Jesus on the Mount of Transfiguration, so heaven has already used these two as special agents! Whatever their identity, however, these men will have a powerful ministry.

In fact, they will so outrage the Antichrist that he will have them executed. The Bible tells us that their bodies will lie where they have fallen, in the streets of Jerusalem, and that all the world will see it.

How could that last part—about the whole world witnessing these events—have even been possible until fairly recently? Today, through satellite technology, nobody even thinks twice about it. The residents of the world could watch it all play out on their TVs, laptops, or cell phones.

As they are watching, however, they will see something that will shock the whole world:

Now after the three-and-a-half days the breath of life from God entered them, and they stood on their feet, and great fear fell on those who saw them. And they heard a loud voice from heaven saying to them, "Come up here." And they ascended to heaven in a cloud, and their enemies saw them. (Revelation 11:11-12)

Wow, talk about must-see TV!

God always has the last word, doesn't He?

But an even greater event follows this. In Revelation 19, we see the return of Christ, which brings the tribulation period to a close.

Now I saw heaven opened, and behold, a white horse. And He who sat on him was called Faithful and True, and in righteousness He judges and makes war. His eyes were like a flame of fire, and on His head were many crowns. He had a name written that no one knew except Himself. He was clothed with a robe dipped in blood, and His name is called The Word of God. And the armies in heaven, clothed in fine linen, white and clean, followed Him on white horses. (Revelation 19:11-14)

It is the Second Coming of Jesus Christ, and here are a few aspects of that occasion we can immediately notice.

The Second Coming of Jesus Christ will be public, and seen by all.

There will be no question in the minds of those witnessing this climactic event. No one will say, "Oh, it's just a bad storm or some kind of atmospheric disturbance." Jesus said, "For the Son of Man in his day will be like the lightning, which flashes and lights up the sky from one end to the other" (Luke 17:24, NIV).

The newspapers won't need to employ their "Second Coming" type. Everyone will see this, and everyone will realize, "This is it."

The Second Coming will be accompanied by sadness and weeping.

The nation of Israel will mourn as they realize that Jesus indeed was and is their Messiah. In Zechariah 12:10, God says:

Then I will pour out a spirit of grace and prayer on the family of David and on all the people of Jerusalem. They will look on me whom they have pierced and mourn for him as for an only son. They will grieve bitterly for him as for a firstborn son who has died. (NLT).

This event, the Second Coming of Jesus, will finally bring an end to the senseless wars of mankind. Humanity will never be able to wipe out terrorism and violence with military and/or political solutions. This will only happen when Christ returns and establishes His kingdom.

Now again, let's understand the difference between the rapture and the Second Coming. At this point, the rapture will have already happened. In fact, it will have happened before the appearance of Antichrist, and before the beginning of the Tribulation.

Notice that it says He comes on a white horse. As we've already noted, His imitator the Antichrist does the same. But this will be the real deal; this will be *Air Horse One!* This will not be the Antichrist wearing a crown; this will be the King of kings and Lord of lords wearing many crowns.

People often wonder what Jesus looked like in His days on earth. In the Second Coming, we know what He will look like. Scripture says that His eyes will like a flame of fire, on His head will be many crowns, and He will have a name written that no one will know except Himself.

Three things stand out in the description of Jesus as He returns in power and glory.

His eyes are like a flame of fire.

When you meet someone for the first time, you look them in the eyes and say, "Hello. It's nice to meet you." I am always suspicious of people who won't make eye contact—who look down or look away. It will be extremely difficult to make eye contact with Jesus at this point, because there will be fire coming out of His eyes. This speaks of His power, His glory, His holiness, and His wrath at this point.

On His head are many crowns.

Why? Because He is Lord over all the uNIVerse.

His robe will be dipped in blood (v. 13).

A better translation might be that His robe will be spattered with blood, reminding us of His death when He came the first time.

It's interesting to contrast the first and second comings of Jesus. In his first coming, when He arrived in that manger in Bethlehem, He was wrapped in swaddling cloths. In His Second Coming, He will be clothed royally, in a robe spattered in blood. In His first coming He was surrounded by animals and shepherds. In His Second Coming He will be accompanied by saints and angels. At His first coming the door of the inn was closed to Him. But in His Second Coming the door of the heavens is opened to Him. The first time He came He was the Lamb of God, dying for the sin of the world. At His Second Coming He is the ferocious Lion of the Tribe of Judah, bringing judgment.

And notice this: When He returns, Jesus will not be alone.

Verse 14 speaks of "the armies of heaven, clothed in fine linen, white and clean" who follow Him on white horses. Who are these armies? They are also mentioned in Jude 14, as the Lord coming with ten thousands of His saints.

Who are these saints who will return with Jesus when He comes to the earth? Colossians 3:4 gives us the answer when it says, "When Christ, who is your life, appears, then you also will appear with him in glory" (NIV).

He will return with His saints, and that is what you are if have received Jesus as your Savior.

Some would say, "Me? Greg, I'm no saint."

You might say such a thing, only because we have misunderstood and misused this biblical term through years. The term has been attributed to someone who performs a miracle—or lived especially an especially holy life and has been canonized by the church.

That may be a church tradition, but it's not what the Bible teaches.

Scripture tells us that if you are a believer, then *you* are a saint. It's just another word for believer. Because of Christ's death on the cross, God has placed the very righteousness of Jesus Christ into my spiritual bank account, and now He regards me as a saint. Not because of what I have done or accomplished, but because of what He accomplished for me in His love and grace.

And on the day that He returns to earth as King of Kings, I will return with him. And so will you, if you belong to Him.

Now how should this affect me? How should I live? What should I be doing in light of the fact that Christ could come for me at any time, and one day I will return with Him to this earth when He establishes His kingdom? To find the answer to those questions we have to shift gears, and consider an eye-opening passage in the book of Luke.

"When You Do Not Expect Him..."

These are the words of Jesus to His people on how we are to live in recognition of the fact that He could come back at any moment.

> Be dressed ready for service and keep your lamps burning, like men waiting for their master to return from a wedding banquet, so that when he comes and knocks they can immediately open the door for him. It will be good for those servants whose master finds them watching when he comes. I tell you the truth, he will dress himself to serve, will have them recline at the table and will come and wait on them. It will be good for those servants whose master finds them ready, even if he comes in the second or third watch of the night. But understand this: If the owner of the house had known at what hour the thief was coming, he would not have let his house be broken into. You also must be ready, because the Son of Man will come at an hour when you do not expect him.

> Peter asked, "Lord, are you telling this parable to us, or to everyone?"

> The Lord answered, "Who then is the faithful and wise manager, whom the master puts in charge of his servants to give them their food allowance at the proper time? It will be good for that servant whom the master finds doing so when he returns. I tell you the truth, he will put him in charge of all his possessions. But suppose the servant says to himself, 'My master is taking a long time in coming,' and he then begins to beat the menservants and maidservants and to eat and drink and get drunk. The master of that servant will come on a day when he does not expect him and at an hour he is not aware of. He will cut him to pieces and assign him a place with the unbelievers." (Luke 12:35-46, NIV)

While this illustration would have been readily understood by people of the first century, it may be a little perplexing to us. Jesus is describing a first century wedding that was way different than our weddings of today.

Today's weddings usually last no longer than an hour or ninety minutes, followed by a reception. But the Jewish weddings of Jesus' day were quite different, and could last for days. One of the elements of those weddings is that no one really knew when the bridegroom would arrive. As a result, everyone would be dressed and ready for his coming. And once the bridegroom showed up, the announcement would be given, "The bridegroom is here" and the wedding would start.

It could happen at 2:00 in the afternoon or 2:00 in the morning. The point was, you needed to be ready because he could come at any moment.

So with this backdrop in mind, everybody understood what Jesus was saying. Jesus says in Luke 12, verse 35 (New King James Version), "So let your waist be girded and your lamps burning." Now what on earth does it mean to gird a waist? As you know, people wore long, flowing robes in those days. And to gird a waist simply meant that you pulled your robe up above your knees and cinched in your belt, giving you freedom of movement.

Another way we could translate this might be, just have your comfortable pants on—or your workout clothes!—and be ready to move. You get the idea. Jesus was simply saying, "Be ready to go at a moment's notice."

And to "have your lamp burning" meant that you would have oil in your lamp. We might say, check to make sure you have fresh batteries for your flashlight. I don't know if you're like me, but I have a number of flashlights around the house that are basically useless to me, because they don't have good batteries in them. That's not wise, because if you need a flashlight, you really need a flashlight, and you want to make sure it's ready to go when the need arises.

Jesus is essentially saying the same thing when he says, "Have your lamps burning." In other words, always be prepared.

In verse 38, the Lord says, "And if he should come in the second watch, or come in the third watch, and find them so [watching for their master], blessed are those servants."

Back in those days the night was divided up into four watches, or shifts. The first watch was from 6:00 to 9:00, the second from 9:00 to 12:00, and the third from 12:00 to 3:00. And the fourth watch of the night was that time right before dawn. So Jesus was effectively saying, "Even if I come later than you originally expected, be ready."

It may seem to us at times that the Lord is delaying His coming, and we wonder why He hasn't come sooner. But the fact is, the Lord is not late. He's right on schedule. He is paying close attention to what is going on in the world today, and He has a day and an hour when He will return.

No one knows that day or the hour. When someone comes along and tells you, "I've got it all figured out! I know the day when He will return," don't believe them.

Bottom line? Don't get into date setting. It's pointless and really quite silly. Just be ready.

The Lord is not late, but He is waiting for people to believe. The apostle Peter said, "The Lord isn't really being slow about his promise to return, as some people think. No, he is being patient for your sake. He does not want anyone to perish, so he is giving more time for everyone to repent" (2 Peter 3:9, NLT).

If He comes in the second watch, the third watch, or even the fourth watch, be ready because we know this much: He *is* coming. We have never been closer to the Lord's return than we are at this very moment.

So what are we to do until then? I'd like to bring a few things to your attention:

We are to be watching for Him.

Luke 12, verse 37 says, "Blessed are those servants whom the master, when he comes, will find watching."

That doesn't mean that we are standing around on street corners staring up into the sky like a bunch of idiots. But what it does mean is that we hold onto the awareness that Christ could return at any time. And when we see the signs of His coming, we're to take note of those things.

When you open up your newspaper or go to your favorite news site on the Web and hear about a another killer quake, or a global currency, or threats to wipe Israel off the face of the earth, or new conflicts breaking out in the Middle East, these are signs of the times. And they should serve as prods or a wake up call to pay attention. We're to be actively waiting and watching for His return.

We are to be ready to go.

When I leave on a trip, I always pack my bag the night before so I can be ready. That's the idea, here. That we, in a sense, would have our bags packed, and sitting close to the door in easy reach. Why? Because we could leave this world at any moment.

So here is a question I ought to ask myself periodically.

When I am about to go to a certain place or do a certain thing, would I be embarrassed if Jesus came back when I was right in the middle of it? If the answer to that question is yes, then it would be best for me to refrain from doing that activity or going to that place.

The truth is, we can study Bible prophesy all day long and can get excited about it, but if it isn't impacting us *in the way that we live*, then we're simply missing the point. In 1 John 3, we read:

> What we know is that when Christ is openly revealed, we'll see him—and in seeing him, become like him. All of us who look forward to his Coming stay ready, with the glistening purity of Jesus' life as a model for our own. (v. 2-3, THE MESSAGE)

Stay ready. Stay steady. Living in the light of Christ's imminent return should make a difference in our behavior. The apostle Peter adds these words:

> When the Day of God's Judgment does come, it will be unannounced, like a thief. The sky will collapse with a thunderous bang, everything disintegrating in a huge conflagration, earth and all its

works exposed to the scrutiny of Judgment.

Since everything here today might well be gone tomorrow, do you see how essential it is to live a holy life? Daily expect the Day of God, eager for its arrival. The galaxies will burn up and the elements melt down that day—but we'll hardly notice. We'll be looking the other way, ready for the promised new heavens and the promised new earth, all landscaped with righteousness.

So, my dear friends, since this is what you have to look forward to, do your very best to be found living at your best, in purity and peace. (I John 3: 10-14, THE MESSAGE)

We should be anxiously awaiting His return.

Anxiously awaiting…not dreading it. I used to have a dog that would sleep outside of my door at night, actually resting his weight against the door. In fact, there were times I would hear knocking in the middle of the night, and think somebody was at the door. But it was only the dog, scratching.

I would know that he had been leaning against the door all night because when I opened it in the morning, he would sort of roll into the room. He would look at me, all excited, as if to say, "Oh, you're up! Good!" He would start going around in circles, singing in his dog mind, "Happy days are here again. The sky is blue! Oh, we are going on a walk. It's so thrilling. Life is good." That's the way he greeted me in the mornings.

It reminds me of that bumper sticker that says, "Lord help me be the person my dog thinks I am." Dogs have so much love and admiration for their masters. Cats? They couldn't care less. With them it's more, "What? You again? I'm leaving for two weeks. See ya."

To shift this out of the animal realm, imagine you were anxiously awaiting the arrival of a close friend whom you hadn't seen for years. You've experienced that, haven't you? You get up every couple of minutes to look out the window. Finally, you see their car pull up and they come walking up to your front door. You open the door before they can even knock, practically pulling them inside.

That is how we should be waiting for the Lord's return. Not with dread, but with joyful, anxious anticipation and excitement. Is that how you feel?

Jesus says, "Behold I come quickly." And we, along with the apostle John, should be able to say in response, "Even so, come quickly Lord Jesus." Anything in our lives that would cast a shadow over that answer is out of place.

That brings us to this final statement of Jesus speaking about His return in Luke 12:

> But if that servant says in his heart, 'My master is delaying his coming,' and begins to beat the male and female servants, and to eat and drink and be drunk, the master of that servant will come on a day when he is not looking for him, and at an hour when he is not aware, and will cut him in two and appoint him his portion with the unbelievers. (vv. 45-46)

Now this is interesting because it says, "The servant says in his heart, 'My master is delaying his coming.'" I think this may be speaking about an individual who appears to be a Christian, but in fact really isn't. In other words, he or she isn't a pagan or a person outside of the church, but an individual who is involved in things of the Lord, to one degree or another.

"My master delays his coming…."

The idea here is that he is not a real servant, and the master is not his real master, but only appears to be.

As I read these words, my concern would be for people in church—even people who seem to be active and involved in church—who are in reality not right with God.

If you come to church with a heart open to God, and a desire to worship and to pray and to hear God's Word and apply it, if you come to church and want to be a part of the body and want to serve the Lord and give to the Lord, then your church will be an oasis for you. A place of refreshment and blessing.

If on the other hand you come to church with a chip on your shoulder, and a hardened heart full of bitterness and criticism, watch out! As has often been noted, the same sun that softens the wax hardens the clay. And that is where church can be dangerous. If you come with a heart that is hard, it can actually become *harder* in the church than perhaps any other place.

Are you ready for the return of Jesus Christ?

Are you prepared for His coming, carefully watching the signs of the times, and longing to see Him?

Jesus says, "Blessed—happy, and to be envied—is that servant whom his master finds so doing when he arrives. Truly I tell you, he will set him in charge of all his possessions" (Luke 12:43-44, AMPLIFIED).

I don't know about you, but that's more than enough motivation for me.

Chapter Six

WHAT EVERY LAST-DAYS-BELIEVER NEEDS TO KNOW

The created world itself can hardly wait for what's coming next. Everything in creation is being more or less held back. God reins it in until both creation and all the creatures are ready and can be released at the same moment into the glorious times ahead.
—*Romans 8:19-20, The Message*

These are certainly days to watch the headlines.

Yes, it's informative to read the articles, too. But even just scanning the headlines alone in your newspaper or on your favorite news website can give you a good idea of the way our world is drifting. You can almost hear our planet's groans and sighs, as it awaits the King who will redeem it.

An article I read recently claimed that Al-Qaeda, the notorious terrorist group that claims responsibilities for the 9-11 attacks against the World Trade Center and the Pentagon, is now on the brink of acquiring nuclear deadly nuclear devices. Quoting certain leaked diplomatic cables, the article said that Al-Qaeda was on the verge producing radioactive weapons—after sourcing nuclear material and recruiting rogue scientists to build "dirty" bombs.[37]

That's a headline that makes you pause, shake your head a little, and maybe whisper, *"Wow. What's next?"*

What are we supposed to do, how are we supposed to respond when we hear things like this? Panic? Give in to anxiety? Fill our garage up to the rafters with emergency supplies?

No, that's not what Jesus said. In Luke 21:28, He declared: "Now when these things begin to happen, look up and lift up your heads, because your redemption draws near."

Don't you like that? We're not to look from side to side, like people who are anxious or nervous, and we're not to look down, like people who are discouraged. We are to look up, as people who know where there help and salvation are coming from.

So here's the question: Now that we've established that we are very likely living in the last days, how are we supposed to live as believers? What sorts of qualities ought to should characterize our attitudes and our lives?

In this chapter, we will check out some of the highlights of Matthew 13, and the Lord's parables concerning the kingdom of God. As Jesus relates some word pictures about the kingdom of God on earth, it helps us to consider how to order our lives in increasingly difficult and anxious times.

Birds, Seeds, and Trees

Another parable He put forth to them, saying: "The kingdom of heaven is like a mustard seed, which a man took and sowed in his field, which indeed is the least of all the seeds; but when it is grown it is greater than the herbs and becomes a tree, so that the birds of the air come and nest in its branches." (Matthew 13:31-32)

Jesus said, "*The kingdom of heaven is like….*"

He didn't say, "The kingdom of heaven IS," He said, "It's *like* this," or maybe, "compare it to this." And the comparison He made was (of all things) to a mustard seed.

Frankly, that doesn't mean a lot to us today. We have French's mustard, deli mustard, hot Chinese mustard—all kinds of mustard, but what in the world is the significance of a mustard seed?

When Jesus walked the earth, however, people of His day would have immediately understood this. A mustard seed was regarded as one of the smallest of all seeds. Jesus Himself called it "the least of all seeds." On another occasion He said, "Even if you had faith as small as a mustard seed…you could say to this mulberry tree, 'May God uproot you and throw you into the sea,' and it would obey you!" (Luke 17:6, NLT).

So the idea here was that a mustard seed was about the smallest thing you could imagine.

Mustard seeds, however, don't grow into trees, as in the parable; they grow into bushes or shrubs. So what Jesus is talking about here wasn't normal growth at all, it was remarkable, supernatural growth. He was saying, "The kingdom of God is like something very, very small that grows into something incredibly—even freakishly—big."

It would be like saying, "The kingdom of heaven is like a Chihuahua that grew to be the size of an elephant." (Interesting thought. Maybe if a Chihuahua really became the size of an elephant, it would stop trembling like a leaf in the wind all the time.) You see, a Chihuahua the size of size of a bus or an elephant would be something way beyond any normal expectation, and that's the idea being conveyed here.

So here is this little bush that grows into a giant tree. What does that mean? One interpretation paints this in a very positive light, reminding us that big trees in Scripture almost always portray something of power and great influence. Nebuchadnezzar was compared to a tree, as was Pharaoh. So the bottom line according to this view is that the church is powerful and influential, impacting the world, and all of the birds come and nest in our branches.

That's one interpretation, but to me, it doesn't line up with other New Testament scriptures. In Luke 18:8, Jesus asks the question, "When the Son of Man comes, will He really find faith on the earth?" As I understand it, I don't believe the Bible teaches that we will create some kind of super church on planet Earth before the Lord's return.

And what about those birds in the parable?

Earlier in Matthew 13, in the parable of the sower, birds are portrayed as a symbol of evil—of the "wicked one" who comes and snatches away the good seed of the Word of God. (Did you ever see Alfred Hitchcock's horror classic *The Birds*? You'll never look at birds exactly the same way again, after seeing that film.)

I believe this is a picture of the church being invaded by imposters in the last days. That certainly fits what we see in the contemporary church scene today. As the Bible predicts, that are many who hold to "a form of godliness," but deny its power.[38]

It's somewhat easy to talk about "the church," because that seems big and vague and not very personal. The true church of Jesus Christ, however, is made up of people, and you are one of those people. And we are all—every one of us—in danger of compromising our faith and our walk with God. Compromise remains one of the most effective weapons in Satan's arsenal.

The devil realizes he probably can't take you down all at once, so he contents himself with destroying you one bite at a time. That's his approach, and that's been his strategy since the first man and woman walked this earth.

Satan doesn't walk up to you and say, "Hey you, I have a plan for your life, and I want you to consider it for a moment. I am thinking you ought to…well, let's see…be unfaithful to your wife. Or how about multiple affairs? Eventually, after trying to make the marriage work, your wife will give up and leave you. That's when you'll start drinking and become a full-blown alcoholic. Or maybe a drug addict—whatever you prefer. And then you can be estranged from her, from your children, ruin your life, slip into despair, and then maybe one day blow your brains out. So that's my plan. What do you say?"

What fool would agree to terms like those?

The devil is much more clever than that. So he comes with just a little bit of compromise, all wrapped up in shiny paper and ribbon. "Hey, you happily married man," he says. "You've done so well! Congratulations are in order. What a good father and loyal husband you've been! But you've been pushing yourself a little too hard, haven't you? You deserve a little break today…you need to loosen up a little, and have a little fun. Go ahead and flirt a little with that attractive woman at the office. It's just a game, isn't it? Or maybe just check out a little pornography on the Internet. Just take a quick peek. What would it hurt? And what's wrong with wandering down to the hotel bar on your business trip for a drink or two? Or why not try this drug—just once? You never have to do it again."

Little things, you see, lead to big things. Small compromises lead to devastating falls.

I'm reminded of the story of the hunter and the bear. The hunter was out in the woods, looking for a bear to kill. As he tromped along through the forest, he saw a large black bear with its back to him. So he raised his rifle to fire.

Suddenly the bear turned around and said to the hunter, "Excuse me. Isn't it better to talk than to shoot?"

"Well," said, the hunter, lowering his rifle a little, "maybe you have a point."

"Tell me," said the bear, "exactly what it is that you want."

"I want a fur coat," the hunter replied, lowering his rifle even more.

"Very good," said the bear. "And I want a full stomach. So let's be sensible, and try to work out a little compromise." So the bear and the hunter disappeared into the forest. A little bit later, the bear emerged alone, with the negotiations apparently successful. Everyone got what they wanted. The bear got a full stomach, and the hunter got a fur coat.

That's how compromise works, and that's how deals with the devil work. You will always find yourself on the losing side.

"A Little Leaven...."

Another parable He spoke to them: "The kingdom of heaven is like leaven, which a woman took and hid in three measures of meal till it was all leavened." (Matthew 13:33)

Again, at first reading, that story may not mean a lot to us today, but it would have been immediately understood by the people of that day.

Leaven is yeast—and yeast has always negative connotations in Scripture. When Moses was giving instructions to the Israelites about the very first Passover, right before they left Egypt, he told them to get rid of all the leaven in their houses, before they celebrated that sacred meal.[39] Picking up on that picture, Paul wrote to the believers in Corinth, who had actually been boasting about welcoming an immoral and compromising believer into their church. They had been saying, in effect, "Look how tolerant and open-minded we are. We've encouraged this guy to come and join us even though he's involved in a twisted relationship."

Paul said, "No! You've messed up with this. That's not the way you should be living." And he told them in 1 Corinthians 5:6 (NIV): "Your boasting is not good. Don't you know that a little yeast works through the whole batch of dough? Get rid of the old yeast that you may be a new batch without yeast—as you really are."

Another translation puts it like this:

> What a terrible thing it is that you are boasting about your purity, and yet you let this sort of thing go on. Don't you realize that if even one person is allowed to go on sinning, soon all will be affected? (TLB)

Yeast, or leaven, represents corruption, infiltration, and compromise. In the pages of Scripture, it invariably represents negative things. Jesus said, "Beware of the leaven of the Pharisees. Beware of the leaven of the Herodians. Beware of leaven."

So you say, "Okay. Great. So I'll get rid of all the yeast in the house."

No, you probably don't have to worry about the yeast in your pantry or throwing out that bread machine you got for Christmas. But there may be other things in your house that you *should* be rid of. This is a picture of compromise in your life—a situation where little things morph into big things. And it happens more quickly than you might imagine.

Have you ever seen a baby rattlesnake? I used to really like snakes, and when I was a boy, I kept them as pets. A junior-sized rattlesnake, however, is every bit as deadly as the full-grown version. In fact, it's venom is more potent than that of an adult. Yes, it's almost cute with its little rattle and sharp, tiny fangs, but it will *kill* you if it gets the chance.

In the same way, we may coddle what we think of as "little sins" in our lives—small compromises that really don't seem to matter very much. We think, "Oh, it's just a little sin. Kinda cute. It's really nothing. They're just small indulgences. Little white lies."

But wait until those baby rattlers suddenly turn around and bite you.

That's the way compromise seeks to work its way into your life, permeating every corner of it.

In Psalm 66:18, the psalmist says, "If I regard iniquity in my heart, the Lord will not hear me" (KJV). What does that mean? It means, "If I hang on to sin in my life, God won't hear my prayers."

Here is my question for you? Is there sin in your life right now that you have never dealt with? Do you imagine to yourself that it's secret, and no one will see or know? Do you think you've covered your steps? Listen to this: Secret sin on earth is open scandal in heaven. There are no secrets with God. He is aware of it—not only of the act, but of all the rationalizing thoughts leading up to it.

What is the secret sin in your life? I don't know what it is. But I know that you know, because right now as you read my words you're thinking about it. And the Lord sees it, just as though it was written over your head in neon.

That act, attitude, or thought could represent compromise in your life. And it could very well be the thing that brings you down. Get rid of that leaven in your life, before it spreads, and eats away your spiritual life and walk with God.

Radical Measures

In April 2003, while doing some solo exploring of the Utah back-country, twenty-eight year old Aron Ralston was rock climbing when an 800-pound boulder suddenly shifted, crushing his right hand and pinning it against the canyon wall. Nothing he tried could dislodge his arm. Days went by, and Ralston was cold, hungry, dehydrated, and beginning to become delirious. He had no cell phone with him, no one knew where he was, and he eventually had to admit to himself that no one would be coming to his aid. Finally, he realized he would die in that place unless he undertook one last, desperate measure.

He would have to cut his own arm off. Just below the elbow. With a cheap, dull knife. And that's just what he did.

It took a long time, and it was very painful. He had to hack his way through skin, muscle, blood vessels, and bone. Amazingly, after he had done the deed, Ralston was able to rappel down a 65-foot sheer cliff, walk out, and live to tell the story.[40]

It was a terrible thing to have to do. But Aron Ralston realized that it would be better to have one arm and be alive, than to have two arms and be dead. A drastic measure? Yes, it was. But that's what it took for this young man to stay alive. He is now married, and the couple has a baby son.

Is there a drastic measure you need to take in your life? Is there an area in your life you need to deal with? Maybe it's a relationship, a certain individual who always drags you down spiritually, whenever you're around him or her. Or maybe it's a certain place where you used to go, certain practices you used to enjoy, or certain habits you used to indulge. But now the Holy Spirit is whispering to you, *Come away from that person. Come away from that place. Turn away from those movies or books or games or music. Cut that thing out of your life. Don't drive down the street near the bar where you used to sit every night, drinking your life away.*

Make a clear choice to turn away from the friendships or habits that drag you down, and cast a shadow over your walk with Jesus Christ.

I was a fairly new Christian when Cathe and I first started dating, and at one point I apparently told her, "If you ever get in the way of my relationship with God, I'm outta here!"

I don't remember saying anything like that, but she says that I did. "Are you sure?" I asked her recently. "I said that?"

"Yes," she affirmed.

"Boy, I was quite the romantic, wasn't I?"

"Oh," she replied, "but I liked it."

"Really?"

"Yes. Because other guys I'd dated always did what I wanted them to do, and I could manipulate them. But you had convictions, and I thought that was a great thing."

Let me just a word to you if you're not yet married. As you look for a mate, make sure you find someone who builds up your faith, rather than tearing it down. Don't even consider a person who isn't a believer as a romantic possibility or a potential mate. More than that, you should be looking for a godly man or woman—someone with whom you can grow in the Lord serve Him together for the rest of your lives.

Treasure and Pearls

> Again, the kingdom of heaven is like treasure hidden in a field, which a man found and hid; and for joy over it he goes and sells all that he has and buys that field.
>
> Again, the kingdom of heaven is like a merchant seeking beautiful pearls, who, when he had found one pearl of great price, went and sold all that he had and bought it. (Matthew 13:44-45)

There are two different ways you could interpret these parables.

One way of looking at this is to say that we are like the person who finds the treasure in the field, or the pearl of great price. And as a result of what we've found, we sell all we have to obtain it. In other words, one day we hear the gospel of Jesus Christ, and we realize it's the most profound, important thing we've ever heard. As a result, we give up everything to follow Christ. He is the treasure hidden in the field; He is the pearl of great price.

That's a valid interpretation, but as I read these parables, I find myself leaning in another direction. Instead of you or me finding that great treasure and giving all we have to purchase it, the other interpretation says that Christ is the person who finds it…and we are the treasure.

In verse 44 we read, "…for joy over it he goes and sells all that he has and buys that field." That reminds me of the story Jesus told in Luke 15, about the shepherd who had a hundred sheep, and one that went astray. After he went out in the wilds and found and rescued that wandering sheep,

> …he joyfully puts it on his shoulders and goes home. Then he calls his friends and neighbors together and says, 'Rejoice with me; I have found my lost sheep.' I tell you that in the same way there will be more rejoicing in heaven over one sinner who repents than over ninety-nine righteous persons who do not need to repent. (vv. 6-7, NIV)

Do you see the theme of joy? Jesus gave up all the privileges of deity, walked among us as a Man, and went to the cross and suffered and died and rose again from the dead. He bought the treasure, He bought the pearl, with His own blood. He gave up all that He had. And He did it for the joy of rescuing us and bringing us Home.

Casting Out the Net

> Once again, the kingdom of heaven is like a net that was let down into the lake and caught all kinds of fish. When it was full, the fishermen pulled it up on the shore. Then they sat down and collected the good fish in baskets, but threw the bad away. This is how it will be at the end of the age. The angels will come and separate the wicked from the righteous and throw them into the fiery furnace, where there will be weeping and gnashing of teeth. (Matthew 13:47-50)

This is the idea of dragging a net through the water, and then sorting out what that net pulls up.

Have you ever seen something like that on TV? The commercial fishermen reel in these massive nets out of the sea into their ship, and the nets are full of all kinds of things. Yes, there are fish, but there may also be a squid, an octopus, a shark—or maybe an old refrigerator or something. They never know what they're going to pull in until they dump the nets in the big bins and start sorting out their catch.

And that's what we're doing in the church—and even in our Harvest Crusades around the world. We're fishing for people and, believe me, we get all kinds.

Will we bring in some bad ones along with the good? Some that won't last?

Of course.

Will we find ourselves with false believers alongside true believers? There's no question about it.

But God knows the secrets of every heart. And He will sort it all out, in His time and His way.

Jesus said, "Follow Me, and I will make you fishers of men." That's our purpose and goal! And that sentence could better be translated, "Follow Me, and you will catch men alive." That particular wording is used in only one other New Testament passage. It's in 2 Timothy where Paul writes, "Then they will come to their senses and escape from the Devil's trap. For they have been held captive by him to do whatever he wants" (2 Timothy 2:26, NLT).

Caught alive by Satan! What a terrible picture.

So one of two things are going to happen to our family members, friends, neighbors, and acquaintances. Either God will catch them alive, give them a full and significant life on earth, and take them to heaven when they die, or Satan will catch them alive, and keep them in darkness as POWs.

Jesus said, in essence, "Let's go fishing for men and women. Let's go catch some people for God's glory." Our job, with the Lord's help, is to keep throwing out that net and pulling it in. You may come up with some junk from the bottom of the sea, or some strange-looking critters, but you'll also bring in some prize catches, as well.

In the Meantime...Press into Purity

If you're driving down the freeway and a state patrol officer pulls up behind you, what's the first thing you usually do? Most often, your eye will go to your speedometer…and you will probably find yourself slowing down. Even if you have your cruise control set exactly at the correct speed limit, you'll probably still brake a little. Why? Because the presence of an officer changes your conduct.

That is how we should view the return of Christ. If we really believe Jesus is coming, it should affect our conduct. Here's how the apostle John put it:

> Yes, dear friends, we are already God's children, right now, and we can't even imagine what it is going to be like later on. But we do know this, that when he comes we will be like him, as a result of seeing him as he really is. And everyone who really believes this will try to stay pure because Christ is pure. (1 John 3:2-3, TLB)

We should be seeking to live godly lives as we await the coming of Jesus.

Thinking back to those verses in the book of Exodus, Moses told the people to get rid of the old leaven in their homes—every bit of it—in preparation for Passover, and in preparation for a journey. The people were about to set out for new lives in the Promised Land, and they needed to clean out their cupboards before they left.

We too, have a journey up ahead. In just a few blinks of the eye, we will be stepping into eternity, either through death or through the coming of the Lord. With that in mind, it's time to get rid of some old things—old habits, old attitudes, old prejudices, old patterns of life—so that we'll be ready for the journey.

Scripture says that Jesus will come in a moment. In the "twinkling of an eye." And those who believe will be caught up to meet the Lord in the air. But not everybody will go in the Rapture. Remember the verses we quoted earlier? Jesus said,

> Two men will be working together in the field; one will be taken, the other left. Two women will be grinding flour at the mill; one will be taken, the other left. So be prepared, because you don't know what day your Lord is coming. (Matthew 24:40-42, NLT)

So here is my question to you. Will you be caught up or will you be left behind?

I hope you are ready.

Chapter Seven

HOT-BUTTON ISSUES

*Every part of Scripture is God-breathed and useful one way or another—showing us
truth, exposing our rebellion, correcting our mistakes, training us to live God's way.
Through the Word we are put together and shaped up for the tasks God has for us.
—2 Timothy 3:16-17, THE MESSAGE*

The Word of God is *always* relevant. Period.

As we take note of the signs of the times, and as they seem to be converging and escalating day by day right before our eyes, we might find ourselves wondering if the Bible will "keep up" with the swift march of events. Everything seems to be changing so fast—technology, the economy, the world situation, attitudes and morals—can we really expect God's Word to keep up with the curve?

Yes, we can.

More than that, we can expect it to be ahead of the curve.

God knew about what would be facing us in the twenty-first century before the first man and first woman ever drew breath in the Garden of Eden. And the Bible will continue to be a reliable handbook and guidebook for our times no matter how quickly the world morphs and changes around us.

Every generation has its "hot button" issues, and ours is no exception.

Is the Bible up to the task of speaking to world events as well as a culture in turmoil? *Absolutely.*

Opposition to a Biblical worldview

Speaking of the Bible and our culture, there used to be a time in our country when the most well-known Bible passages among all people was either John 3:16 or Psalm 23.

Now, the non-believer's favorite verse is Matthew 7:1. Granted, they may not know that the reference is from the gospel of Matthew, or the context in which these words were spoken. They may or may not know that Jesus Himself spoke the words. They just happen to like what it says—or, at least, what they think it says.

"Judge not, lest you be judged."

This is usually quoted about the time you say something they consider "judgmental." (Which might be defined as an absolute opinion on any subject they disagree with. Where you would dare to say something as controversial and unkind as, "No, that's wrong!")

The response is usually pretty heated. *"Who are YOU to judge ME? Doesn't the Bible say 'Judge not lest you be judged?'"*

By the way, that verse isn't saying we shouldn't judge; it's saying we shouldn't *condemn*. And no true believer in Jesus should do that. The fact is, I think true Christians are among the most loving, the most open, and the most accepting people anywhere. I find the most narrow-minded people are the ones who claim to be broad-minded.

Those who claim to be the most accepting are in reality the most un-accepting. A true Christian bases his or her ideas and opinions on a Biblical worldview. Non-believers will also have their opinions, based on a secular worldview. Ironically, they will say that they have no world view, but they really do. They will say they are open to everything, but in reality they are quite closed.

Everyone has a right to their opinion today except the one with the biblical worldview. They would rather we just went away quietly, and didn't express our opinion at all.

For instance…a typical statement of a person with a non-biblical worldview might be, "All religions essentially teach the same thing."

Actually, they don't. A person says that reveals his or her complete ignorance of the matter. This is illustrated in the *mea culpa* of golf icon Tiger Woods some time ago. After acknowledging personal responsibly for his multiple infidelities, he went on to say that he had actively practiced his faith from childhood, but "obviously, I lost track of what I was taught."[41]

That faith is Buddhism.

The problem with Buddhism is they do not believe in a personal God who is capable of loving you or forgiving you for your sins.

I can hear someone respond: "That's insensitive and unkind to say that! Who are you to judge and say something mean about Buddhists?"

But that statement isn't mean at all. It's what Buddhists themselves say about their own faith. A Buddhist in New York City said, "Many Buddhists do *not* believe in a personal God, and there is no one to forgive you." A director of a Buddhist meditation center in New York City said, "If redemption is defined as being forgiven by a God that is outside of ourselves, Buddhists don't believe in a god that's outside of ourselves."[41]

That is a *huge* difference from Christianity. Christianity teaches there is a indeed a personal God who can and will forgive because of the sacrifice of Jesus Christ on the cross.

Stephen Prothero, a Boston UNIVersity professor on Buddhism, told the press: "You have a law of Karma, so no matter what Woods says or does, he is going to have to pay for whatever wrongs he's done. There's no Accountant in the sky wiping sins of your balance sheet, like there is in Christianity."[42]

Accountant in the sky?

Our sins were removed by the voluntary death of Jesus on the cross for us.

When Fox News commentator Brit Hume dared to suggest that Tiger turn to Christ, there was outrage across the board. In a panel discussion, Hume said of Tiger: "He is said to be a Buddhist. I don't think that faith offers the kind of forgiveness and redemption that is offered by the Christian faith. So my message to Tiger would be, 'Tiger, turn to the Christian faith and you can make a total recovery and be a great example to the world.'"[42]

That's called a Christian worldview.

One commentator huffed, "The fact that a journalist—and I use that term loosely as it pertains to Hume—would go on a national news show and put down another high-profile individual's faith should tell all of us that religious bigotry, and bigotry as a whole, is a growing problem in this country."[42]

But why is it "bigotry" to express an opinion about your faith? That's what Christians are all about—we try to convince people to believe in Jesus. Why do we do that? *Because Jesus Christ has forgiven and changed us, and we want to help others.*

In the process, of course, we welcome people of other faiths to express theirs as well. We don't kill them or try to silence them. We listen to them, and try to bring them to Jesus.

It's all about your worldview: a biblical worldview simply means that you are learning how to think and live in accordance with the teachings of the Bible.

When it comes to discussing some of the more "hot button" issues of our time, then, it is important that we learn to respond in a *biblical* way, rather than responding in an emotional or coldly-logical way.

Sometimes you will hear people get angry and say, "Well, my God would never say that or do that…." And so on.

But there is only one God, and that is the God of the Bible, the God of Abraham, Isaac and Jacob. This is the very same God who loved us so much He sent His Son Jesus to die for our sin.

"Well, *my* Bible says…."

Actually, your Bible says the same thing that mine says. There is only one true Word of God, and that is the Bible. The debate must start and end there. Otherwise, we will go astray in our thinking, and we will not have a biblical worldview.

In his book *Think Biblically*, Dr. John MacArthur writes that a biblical worldview is based on two major suppositions:

> The first will be the eternal existence of the personal, transcendent, triune, Creator God. Second, the God of Scripture has revealed His character, purposes, and will in the infallible and inerrant pages of His special revelation, the Bible, which is superior to any other source of revelation or human reason alone.[43]

To put that in a more simple way: *There is a living God, and He has revealed Himself in Scripture.* As Christians, therefore, we believe we have absolute truth from God, and we develop our worldview from what the Bible teaches. Period.

We do not seek to conform and accommodate the unchanging truths of Scripture to our changing culture, but rather seek to change our culture to conform to what the Bible teaches.

The Traditional Family

Here is a truth you can hang your life on: *There is a living God, and He has revealed Himself in Scripture.*

As Christians, we believe we have absolute truth from God, and we develop our worldview from what the Bible teaches. We do not seek to conform and accommodate the unchanging truths of Scripture to our changing culture, but rather seek to change our culture to conform to what the Bible teaches.

With these things in mind, we can ready ourselves to discuss some of the more controversial, "hot-button" issues in our culture today.

The Ten Commandments, you may remember, can be divided into two sections. The first four deal with man's relationship with God, and the second six speak to man's relationship with man. It is that second grouping of commandments in Exodus 20 that will speak most clearly to our "hot button" issues.

Verse 12: *"Honor your father and mother…."*

Isn't it interesting? Before a word is spoken about how to treat others, God starts with the family.

Few things in life can give us as much pleasure as our families.

Then again, few things in life can give us as much pain as our families! Kids' have problems with parents. Parents have problems with kids. And on it goes.

Nevertheless, both the Old Testament and New Testament are very clear. Colossians 3:20-21 says, "Children obey your parents in all things, for this is well pleasing to the Lord." Or as the Phillips translation puts it, "And you children, your duty is to obey your parents, for at your age this is one of the best things you can do to show your love for God."

That doesn't mean it both parents and kids won't struggle with this. Sometimes kids will look at their parents and think they don't know what they are talking about. *"How could you say that to me? Why won't you let me do this thing? What is wrong with you?"*

Mark Twain once wrote: "When I was boy of fourteen, my father was so ignorant I could hardly stand to have the old man around. But when I got to be twenty-one, I was astonished by how much he'd learned in seven years."[44]

I'm reminded of a magazine article I read years ago, the describes how a child see their parents as the years pass. And this was specifically about Dad.

At four years old the child says, "My daddy can do anything."
At seven they say, "My daddy knows a lot. A whole lot."
At eight they say, "My father doesn't know quite everything."
At twelve they say, "Dad is so out of date."
At fourteen, "Dad is so lame."
At twenty-five, "Dad know a little bit about it, but not too much."
At thirty, "Let's go find out what Dad thinks about that."
At thirty-five, "Well, before we decide, let's get Dad's idea first."
At fifty, "I wonder what my dad would have thought about that."
And at sixty, "You know what? My dad knew literally everything."

Perhaps you would ask the question, "What if my parents aren't Christians, and don't live God-honoring lives? Should I still honor them?" The answer is yes, you should. The Scripture says, "Honor your father and mother," and there were no qualifiers attached to that command. In fact, your willingness to honor them might be the way you will eventually lead them to the Lord.

We hear so much talk about "dysfunctional families" or "dysfunctional marriages" these days.

I guess I could speak to that because…I came from a dysfunctional family and you might say that I am the head of a dysfunctional family. It seems I have some "irreconcilable difference" with my wife of thirty-eight years. Just consider….

She is neat, and I am messy.

She is sometimes late, and I am usually early.

She is cute, and I am fat.

These are "irreconcilable differences," because she just keeps getting cuter and I keep getting fatter!

The fact is, God starts with the family because He created it! Our very existence as a society is contingent on the success of the family. And that also explains why Satan hates it so, and has declared war on it. It has been said, "A family can survive without a nation, but a nation cannot survive without the family."

Respect for parents is certainly something we have lost sight of in our culture. In fact, this very lack of respect is one of the clear biblical signs that we are in the last days. Paul wrote of those days: *"For men will be lovers of themselves, lovers of money, boasters, proud, blasphemers, disobedient to parents…"* (2 Timothy 3:2).

It's a sign of the times, and there's no doubt about it.

Note that God's command says, "Honor your father and mother," not, "honor your father and father" or "honor your mother and mother" or "honor your mother and her live-in-lover or partner."

We tamper with God's order at our own peril!

There is a movement afoot to "redefine" marriage and family. Media and modern culture are pushing for same-sex marriage and the so-called normalization of homosexuality.

You will hear this most often defined as mere political issue, but don't be misled. It is a *moral* issue and it is a *biblical* issue.

"But if two people are in love in a committed relationship why shouldn't they marry?"

I could reply to that statement in a number of different ways, but here is what counts: *homosexuality is outside of God's order for life*. He did not bring "Adam and Steve" together in the Garden, but Adam and Eve. His pattern is (and always will be) one man, one woman, married for life.

God is not "anti-gay," He is "anti-sin," no matter how it is expressed. He also loves all people, and wants them to come to repentance.

As long as I've put together a controversial chapter here, I would like to highlight the following statement: No one was "born gay," and alcoholism is *not* "a disease."

I get letters for making statements like that. People will say, "That is so insensitive. That is so mean. That is so harsh. That is so judgmental." Actually, it is so biblical. The fact is, you were not born gay, but you were born a sinner. And I will acknowledge that as a person who was born with a sinful nature, you might find yourself attracted to members of the same sex. Certainly that can happen. And I would also acknowledge that as a person who is born a sinner might be more prone to issues of addiction. There are certain people who are perhaps more vulnerable in those areas.

Nevertheless, all of these things, homosexuality, alcoholism, and drug addictions, can be overcome by the power of the Holy Spirit. I have met people who were once addicts, but now live under the control of the Holy Spirit, and no longer are. I have met people who were homosexuals who are now living a happy and fulfilled heterosexual lifestyle, by the power of the indwelling Holy Spirit.

How do you stop being gay if you were "born that way"?

The question is based on a false premise. You *weren't* born that way. You were born a sinner in need of a Savior. And that Savior, Jesus Christ the Lord, can change you and transform you from the inside out, and help you to live the very life He has called you to live.

I can hear someone say, "You are homophobic to say that!" But we could just as easily say, "You are *bibliaphobic* for denying this." (If you dare to speak out against any sin, you are branded something-phobic.)

Here is what God says about sin and sinners not entering His kingdom:

> Don't you know that those who do wrong will have no share in the Kingdom of God? Don't fool yourselves. Those who indulge in sexual sin, who are idol worshipers, adulterers, male prostitutes, homosexuals, thieves, greedy people, drunkards, abusers, and swindlers—none of these will have a share in the Kingdom of God. (1 Corinthians 6:9-10, NLT)

The Bible does not give a confused statement on this topic. There is no confusion on this issue—unless your confusion is with the Bible itself. The apostle Paul in no uncertain terms establishes homosexuality as a sin in Romans 1:22-27.

Here is the heart of that passage:

> That is why God abandoned them to their shameful desires. Even the women turned against the natural way to have sex and instead indulged in sex with each other. And the men, instead of having normal sexual relationships with women, burned with lust for each other. Men did shameful things with other men and, as a result, suffered within themselves the penalty they so richly deserved. (vv. 26-27)

How clear is that? It's very, very clear, and you can either accept it or reject it. But if you reject it, God already spells out the consequences in this first chapter of Romans.

God's order is for the family to be a man and woman, as husband and wife. And even though our culture seems to be doing everything in its power to mock, denigrate, attack, and deny the veracity of that basic relationship, God's truth stands. We must respect the institution of marriage, and give it the honor it deserves.

How I thank God for the couples who have hung in there through life's ups and downs, who have stayed together and raised their children. Their commitments and their sacrifices will have an impact for *generations* to come.

When I was a young boy, coming from a home of divorce was considered scandalous. Now, coming from a home where parents are still together is considered curious! When I tell someone my wife and I have been married for thirty-eight years they are flabbergasted.

The Hebrew word here for "Honoring" your mom and dad comes from a verb that means "to be heavy, so that we give weight." In other words, give your parents the recognition they deserve for their God-given authority. Respect, esteem, value, and prize fathers and mothers as gifts from God.

The fact is, as you get older, you get to see a lot of human drama played out in "real time." You not only see the choices people make when they're younger, but many of the consequences they reap for those decisions when they are older. You see what happens in the lives of people who disregard God's Word. You also see what happens in a culture when many people disregard those changeless truths.

By the same token, however, you also get to see what happens to those who have walked with God and obeyed His Word through the years, and the blessings that follow. That is not to say the Christian life is a "bed of roses." Far from it. Believers indeed suffer and experience tragedy, as my family and I know only too well.

Through it all however, those who cling to God's Words and God's ways, always experience God's faithfulness.

Living in an Anti-Life Culture

Commandment number six of the Ten Commandments says: *"You must not kill"* (Exodus 20:13).

If ever there was a commandment that's being ignored, it is this one. We live in such a violent and murderous culture today. Our society is awash in brutality and bloodshed. Nearly two million people a year in the United States become victims of violent crimes.

A more accurate translation of Exodus 20:13 would read, "You shall not commit murder." This commandment obviously forbids the taking of another human life for no justifiable reason.

No, the Bible does not condemn *all* killing. Numbers 35 plainly states the difference which God sets between killing and murder. All murder, of course, is killing, but not all killing is necessarily murder. There are times when death is permissible (though not desirable).

Self defense is one example. If someone were to break into your home with the intent of killing you or your family, Scripture allows you to defend yourself. At one point, Jesus told the disciples to "take a sword" with them. Why a sword? For shish-kabob? No, for self defense! (Luke 22:36-38)

When our military or law enforcement officers strike at terrorists who have attacked our nation, that is justifiable killing. It is not murder, it is national self defense.

Some pacifists will say, "When we kill terrorists we're just as bad as they are, because all killing is sin." This is called the "moral equivalency" approach. I would respond with this question: Was it wrong to use force to stop the Nazis from destroying the Jews? No, it was a just use of force to save innocent lives.

God has established order and laws by which a culture ought to be governed. There will always be those who break those laws, and there must be repercussions.

The New Testament declares that God Himself has raised up the military and the police to do His work. In Romans 13, the apostle Paul writes:

> For the authorities do not frighten people who are doing right, but they frighten those who do wrong. So do what they say, and you will get along well. The authorities are sent by God to help you. But if you are doing something wrong, of course you should be afraid, for you will be punished. The authorities are established by God for that very purpose, to punish those who do wrong. (vv. 3-4, NLT)

What does the Bible mean when it says, "You shall not murder"? The Hebrew term means "to dash in pieces." It is never used to describe the death of an animal, an opponent in war, or capital punishment. Speaking of capital punishment, it was established by God Himself, many years before the Ten Commandments. Way back in the early

chapters of the book of Genesis, God said: "Murder is forbidden…
any person who murders must be killed. Yes, you must execute anyone who murders another person, for to kill a person is to kill a living
being made in God's image" (Genesis 9:5, 6, NLT).

The Bible consistently views capital punishment as "justice," not
"murder." It is seen as a deterrent to others committing such crimes
of violence, and thus, a protector of life.

In our culture today, groups of people will almost always gather
outside a facility where a person is scheduled to be executed. They
will hold a vigil, sing, pray, light candles, and a few of them will be
carrying signs that say, "Thou shalt not kill."

Some would have difficulty understanding why Christians with a
Biblical worldview would condone the execution of a murderer, and
yet oppose abortion. To me, the opposite view is much more illogical
and difficult to understand: Why in the world do some people oppose
capital punishment, and yet support abortion!

They want to kill the innocent and spare the guilty. I want to spare
the innocent, and judge the guilty.

When it comes to the topic of abortion, deliberately taking the life
of a pre-born baby, there can be no debate. If you believe the Word
of God, you can draw no other conclusion than this: *life begins at
conception.*

Listen to David's words to God as he spoke about being in the
womb:

You made all the delicate, inner parts of my body
and knit me together in my mother's womb.
Thank you for making me so wonderfully complex!
Your workmanship is marvelous—and how well I know it.
You watched me as I was being formed in utter seclusion,
as I was woven together in the dark of the womb.
You saw me before I was born.
Every day of my life was recorded in your book.
Every moment was laid out
before a single day had passed.
(Psalm 139:13-16, NLT)

In another passage, the Bible again shows that God has a plan for each of us, *before our birth*. In Jeremiah 1:5, God declares: "I knew you before I formed you in your mother's womb. Before you were born I set you apart and appointed you as my spokesman to the world."

Notice that God says, "I formed you in your mother's womb." Each child, then, is created by God and should be given the chance to live. God does *not* say, "I waited until you were born to have a plan for you, because you weren't a viable human being yet, but only a mass of tissue."

Max Lucado puts it like this: "You were deliberately planned, specially gifted, and lovingly positioned on this earth by the Master Craftsman."[45]

I was conceived out of wedlock myself. I wasn't planned. In the eyes of my parents, I wasn't meant to be. But I am so grateful that my mom didn't get an abortion, as she easily could have done. In spite of the fact that I was "inconvenient," I was brought to term and allowed to live my life.

Every child has a right to live.

"Well," someone may say, "what about the mother's rights?"

The mother's right is to protect her unborn child, because there are no illegitimate children. Every child is legitimate in the eyes of God, no matter how they were conceived.

Despite this strong biblical affirmation of life, abortion is still used as a form of birth control in our country. Since the passing of Roe vs. Wade in the early 1970s, over 50 million babies have been aborted. I wonder if one of those babies would have grown up to find the cure for cancer…or become the President of the United States…or would have been a great and gifted preacher of the gospel.

We will never know, because they were silenced—killed in the very womb that God intended as the place of nurture and protection. And in the meantime, abortion has grown into a 500 million dollar a year industry in the United States alone. Worldwide, the abortion industry rakes in 10 billion annually.

And here is something that is rarely discussed. Girls or young women who get abortions experience a much higher depression rate than other girls, and attempt suicide far more often than those who did not get an abortion.

Abortion is not the answer. If you have conceived a child and it is possible, marry the father and raise the child. If you can't do that, then raise the child as a single mother. If you can't do that, then carry the child to term and give it up for adoption.

You see all sorts of strange terminology used to describe pre-born babies. People call them "fetuses." Or "embryos." Or maybe "globs of cells," "uterine contents," or "products of conception." And here's my favorite: We hear the term, "potential human beings."

Potential humans? Oh really? What else would they become? Horses? Beavers? Hyenas? No, the child in the womb is not a potential human being, he or she is a human being. A pre-born human being.

In fact, it is a human being with incredible potential.

A human being made in the image of the living God.

Chapter Eight
ANGELS & DEMONS

Bless the Lord, you His angels,
Who excel in strength, who do His word,
Heeding the voice of His word.
—Psalm 103:20

There is an invisible world.

It's difficult for us to believe and accept that, sometimes, because we live in the natural world. We relate to what we can see, hear, taste, smell, or touch. Even so, the Bible teaches that there is an invisible, supernatural world, the realm of God and Satan, and of angels and demons. And it is all around us.

Right now if we could somehow pull back the veil, it would blow our minds to see what we would see. To see the angels of God at work. To see the demons of hell at work. To see all the spiritual activity swirling around us at any given moment.

The book of Second Kings gives us a glimpse of these unseen realities in an illuminating account of the prophet Elisha, and his servant, Gehazi. They were in an Israelite town called Dothan, when Gehazi got up one morning and saw to his horror that the whole town was ringed about by enemy soldiers. In a panic, Gehazi ran to wake up his master with the news.

"What are we going to do?" he wailed.

We can imagine Elisha sitting up in bed and wiping the sleep out of his eyes, trying to digest this information. Apparently, it didn't take him long, because we read these words:

> So he [Elijah] answered, "Do not fear, for those who are with us are
> more than those who are with them." And Elisha prayed, and said,
> "Lord, I pray, open his eyes that he may see." Then the Lord opened the
> eyes of the young man, and he saw. And behold, the mountain was full
> of horses and chariots of fire all around Elisha. (2 Kings 6:16-17)

"Open his eyes…."

And if our spiritual eyes could be opened for a moment or two, we
too would see the angelic forces of God, surrounding us and protect-
ing us. Right along with Elisha we can say, "Those who are with us are
more than those who are with them."

A recent *Time* magazine article revealed that a whopping 69 percent
of Americans believe in the existence of angels, and 48 percent believe
they have their own guardian angel. And 32 percent even said they had
felt some kind of angelic presence in their life at some point.[46]

These statistics show us again that in a broad sense, we are a spiritual people, and believe in an unseen, supernatural world.

Many of us believe in angels because we've sensed an angelic presence in some close brush with death. We've lived through a moment
where we could have been easily killed—in an accident, on the job, or
maybe in a car or motorcycle. And when it was over, after our pound-
ing heart slowed down a little, we couldn't help wondering: Did an
angel intervene on my behalf?

Questionable Sources

Many, if not most, Americans have picked up a lot of our information
and impressions about angels from television and Hollywood.

And that's not good.

Over the years, Hollywood has hijacked the topic of angels, which
has led to some significant distortions (to say the least).

We might think of the angel Clarence, trying to earn his wings
by helping Jimmy Stewart in the holiday favorite, *It's a Wonderful
Life*. Or maybe we caught several episodes of that old TV program,

Touched by an Angel. In a movie called *The Preacher's Wife*, Whitney Houston's character is visited by an angel portrayed by Denzel Washington. In the movie *City of Angels*, Nicholas Cage plays an angel who falls in love with Meg Ryan. In the end, he decides to give up his rights as an angel and become a human.

As a result, we acquire strange ideas that angels are exalted humans, or have to earn their wings, or any number of off-the-wall beliefs, to the point that we really don't know what we believe about angels.

In fact, there is only one reliable source of information on God, Satan, angels, and demons, and that is the Scripture. And as it turns out, the Bible actually has quite a bit to say about these things.

Angels on Task

The activity of angels, especially in the lives of believers, is constant. We may not necessarily be aware of the presence of angels, or be able to predict how and where they might appear, but the Bible says that we can count on the fact that they're there—and perhaps nearer to our daily lives and doings than we might have imagined.

In Psalm 34:7, "For the angel of the LORD encamps around those who fear him, and he delivers them" (NIV).

Did you know that there are at least 300 references to angels in the Old and New Testaments? In these passages, God pulls back the curtain a little and allows us to see angels at work in the lives of believers.

A good example is when Simon Peter was arrested for preaching the gospel in the book of Acts, chapter 12. The passage tells us that the church was earnestly praying for him. In answer to the church's fervent prayers, God dispatches an angel to deliver the imprisoned apostle. Peter, however, is so deep in his sleep that the angel has to practically shake him and punch him to wake him up and get him moving. After that, the heavenly rescuer leads Peter right through the prison doors and gates (that open automatically for them) and leads him out into the street, a free man.

That's the way it is in example after Biblical example. When we cry out to God in a time of danger or distress, He might choose to dispatch an angel to help us.

I love the story in the book of Genesis where Jacob is on his way home, and scared spitless about meeting up with his estranged brother Esau. The Bible says: "Jacob went on his way, and the angels of God met him. When Jacob saw them, he said, 'This is God's camp.' And he called the name of that place Mahanaim (or, two camps)" (Genesis 32:1-2).

If we could only see, we would understand that we're *always* in God's camp.

Angels are amazing creatures, immortal, and sometimes traveling between heaven and earth. In Luke 20:36, Jesus said of people who have gone on to heaven: "…Nor can they die anymore, for they are equal to the angels and are sons of God, being sons of the resurrection."

Angels have a special work to accomplish in the lives of believers. We know that because Hebrews 1:14 tells us, "Are they not all ministering spirits sent forth to minister for those who will inherit salvation?" Many of us who have been believers for years have heard story after story of the work of angels in believers' lives.

First Person Accounts

I'm reminded of a contemporary account from Billy Graham's classic book, *Angels: God's Secret Agents*. In that book, Billy tells the story of John Patton, who was a missionary to the New Hebrides Islands. On one particular night, Patton and his wife were in their home at the mission station and got word of an imminent attack by people who were indigenous to that region, who wanted to kill them.

Knowing this, John and his wife began to pray. Hours passed, however, and all was peaceful; no attack ever came. The next morning there was no sign of their enemies, and the missionaries wondered what had happened.

A year or so later, the chief of the tribe that had wanted to kill the Pattons received Jesus Christ as his Savior. On one occasion John was having a conversation with this chief and said, "I have to ask you what happened that night when you were coming to kill us. Why didn't you follow through on it?" The chief replied, "What do you mean, why didn't we go through with it? Who were all of those men there with you?"

"There were no men there," Patton replied.

But the chief would have none of it. "We didn't attack," he said, "because there were hundreds of big men in shining garments with drawn swords, circling the mission station."

And in that moment, John knew that he and his wife had been guarded by a contingent of angels.[47]

I would even take this subject of encounters with angels a step further, and say that it's entirely possible that you have personally met an angel. We are told in Hebrews 13:1-2: "Keep on loving each other as brothers. Do not forget to entertain strangers, for by so doing some people have entertained angels without knowing it."

Now if I knew I was entertaining an angel, I would definitely take good care of him, wouldn't you?

"Hi. I'm an angel from God. Can you take me to lunch?"

"Yes, certainly. Where would you like to go?"

But what if the Lord sent someone to me who wasn't the kind of a person I would necessarily want to hang around with? What if he sent an unattractive or a difficult person, of the sort I wouldn't normally be inclined to help?

I've often thought about that.

While angels aren't human and have never been human, they sometimes take on human form, appearing as young men. By the way, there is no instance in the Bible of an angel appearing as a woman. In other words (and I'm sorry to tell you this), there are no girl angels.

It's funny, because our culture loves to use that expression "angel" in a feminine sense. We'll say, "Oh, she is pretty as an angel," or, "She sings like an angel." And often in religious art through the years angels have been portrayed as female. In the Bible, however, when they take on a human form, it's always male.

I've always liked Billy Graham's book title, identifying angels with the designation of "God's secret agents." In other words, they're an elite fighting force, like the Navy Seals. When the Seals are dispatched on a mission, they go in, take care of business, and you never hear about it. It's not publicized. You don't know the names of the Seals that did thus and so. You may read about the success of a given mission, but you never learn any of the details.

Like the Seals, angels are sent out on missions all the time. They are "ministering spirits," who protect, deliver, guide, and bring messages from God. You don't need to engage them, and you don't need to try to communicate with them. Just step back and let them do their jobs, the work that God has called them to do.

I think we would be stunned beyond words if we could see how often (and how many) angels become involved in our day-to-day lives.

As you're no doubt aware, 3-D movies have made a big comeback. Not long ago, Cathe and I went to see an animated 3-D movie with our daughter-in-law and our granddaughter, Stella. When we put those 3-D glasses on Stella and she saw those things coming at her from the screen, she started screaming, pulled off the glasses, and wouldn't watch the movie.

My wife and my daughter-in-law took her out to the lobby, but I wanted to stay and watch the movie! I was totally engrossed.

What if we could put on 3-D glasses or 4-D glasses that would allow us to see into the spiritual dimension, and watch angels and demons at work? It would be glorious, yes, but also terrifying.

In fact if an angel were to appear before you at this very moment, your temptation would be to worship him, because he would be so glorious and magnificent. That's exactly what happened to the apostle John on the island of Patmos. (And this is a guy you'd think would know better!)

The book of Revelation tells us that when John encountered one of God's angels, he fell at the angel's feet to worship him. But the angel quickly warned him, "Do not do it! I am a fellow servant with you and with your brothers who hold to the testimony of Jesus. Worship God!"(Revelation 19:10, NIV).

This is a particularly interesting passage, because it underlines the fact that angels don't like to draw attention to themselves, seeking to shift the focus back to God, where it always belongs.

Tread Very Carefully

Even so, our culture has what you might call an obsession with angels. Go into any bookstore and you see book after book about them. Just recently I went to Amazon.com and typed in the keyword "angel." It seemed to me that a lot of these books that came up had an unbiblical approach to this topic.

The trouble with being so interested in contacting angels and talking to angels is that you might end up with the wrong kind of angel—a fallen one, otherwise known as a demon. That's why the apostle said, "But even if we, or an angel from heaven, preach any other gospel to you than what we have preached to you, let him be accursed" (Galatians 1:8).

Why would an angel bring a message contrary to the gospel? Because he would be a fallen angel. Satan, the devil himself, is a fallen angel. He used to be a magnificent, powerful, high-ranking angel who had access to the presence of God, but he rebelled against the Lord and became the adversary of God and humanity. But Scripture tells us that he's kept his old clothes; he can still appear as an "angel of light"(2 Corinthians 11:14).

If the devil were to appear to you today (God forbid!), he would not have red skin, horns, and a pointed tail, carrying a little pitchfork. That is a caricature. The real devil, originally named Lucifer, or "son of the morning," was a magnificent being. (More about that in the pages to come.)

So we must be very, very careful. When people tell you they've had contact with angels, they might very well be listening to the wrong kind of angel, opening themselves up to dangerous demonic influence.

How many angels are out there?

More than we could probably even count.

In the book of Daniel, the prophet speaks in terms of "thousands upon thousands," and "ten thousand times ten thousand." (Daniel 7:10) The book of Revelation uses the same terminology.

Angels are not only numerous, they are very powerful. Psalm 103:20 tells us that they "excel in strength." Angels aren't as powerful as God, but they are vastly more powerful than people. And it would appear that some angels are mightier than others.

There are also rankings among the angels. In 1 Peter 3:22, we read that Jesus Christ has gone into heaven and is at God's right hand "with angels, authorities, and powers in submission to Him." That same ranking, I would assume, also applies to fallen angels. Paul warns us, "We do not wrestle against flesh and blood, but against principalities, against powers, against the rulers of the darkness of this age, against spiritual hosts of wickedness in the heavenly places" (Ephesians 6:12).

The angels of God are organized under the command of the Lord Jesus Christ; the fallen angels are organized under the command of Lucifer, the fallen angel.

There are only three angels that we know for sure by name. One is Michael, the other is Gabriel, and the third is Lucifer, who became Satan. Let's look at these named angels a little more closely.

Michael

Michael is identified in the New Testament book of Jude, verse 9, as "the archangel." Does that mean there are no other archangels? Possibly. The term archangel occurs twice in the New Testament, and in both instances it is used in the singular and is preceded by the definite article *the*. As in, *the* archangel. So there may only be one.

It's interesting that he will play a unique role in the rapture of the church. In 1 Thessalonians 4:16-17, we read: "For the Lord Himself will descend from heaven with a shout, with the voice of an archangel, and with the trumpet of God. And the dead in Christ will rise first. Then we who are alive and remain shall be caught up together with them in the clouds to meet the Lord in the air."

We also know that Michael is called in when lower ranking angels need help. There is a fascinating story in Daniel chapter 10, where the prophet was praying, and the Lord dispatched an angel with an answer to his prayer. After quite a delay, the angel finally showed up and said these words:

> Then he said to me, "Do not fear, Daniel, for from the first day that you set your heart to understand, and to humble yourself before your God, your words were heard; and I have come because of your words. But the prince of the kingdom of Persia withstood me twenty-one days; and behold, Michael, one of the chief princes, came to help me…." (vv. 12-13)

To paraphrase: "Daniel I have to tell you why there seems to be a delay in the answer to your prayer. I was dispatched from heaven twenty-one days ago with an answer, but I was opposed by a powerful fallen spirit identified as the Prince of Persia. I couldn't handle him, so Michael came and overpowered that demon entity, and I was free to then come and bring you the answer to your prayer."

What a fascinating account. And it underlines the fact that there is ranking among angels, and that some are more powerful than others. (Michael, it seems, is *very* powerful.) But it also reminds us that when we pray, our prayers may unleash an invisible spiritual battle, and that the so-called delay to your prayer is due to angelic battles going on behind the scenes.

Please hear this: When you are praying for someone's salvation, when you are praying for a prodigal son or daughter to repent, *don't give up*. You have no idea what is happening behind the scenes, in the spirit world, as you pray. Don't assume that God is saying no to your prayer because the answer doesn't come quickly. He might be saying "no" today, but maybe He will say "yes" tomorrow, or the day after. Just keep praying!

Jesus said, "Ask, and it shall be given you; seek, and ye shall find; knock, and it shall be opened unto you" (Luke 11:9 KJV). A more accurate translation of the original language, however, has this sense: *Keep on* asking. *Keep on* seeking. *Keep on* knocking. God's delays are not necessarily His denials.

We also know that Michael ultimately overcomes Satan himself, as revealed in Revelation 12, where the apostle John speaks about a war in heaven.

> And there was war in heaven. Michael and his angels fought against the dragon, and the dragon and his angels fought back. But he was not strong enough, and they lost their place in heaven. The great dragon was hurled down—that ancient serpent called the devil, or Satan, who leads the whole world astray. He was hurled to the earth, and his angels with him. (vv. 7-9, NIV)

So ultimately, Michael the archangel overcomes Lucifer the fallen angel.

Gabriel

Now Gabriel, though maybe not an archangel, is certainly a high ranking one. Gabriel appears in both the Old and New Testaments. In Daniel, he appears to the prophet with a revelation of the future. At the beginning of the new covenant, he appears to Zechariah and tells him he is going to be the father of the last of the Old Testament prophets—John the Baptist, the direct forerunner of the Messiah.

Gabriel was also given the privilege of appearing to a young girl named Mary living in Nazareth, to tell her she would be the mother of the Messiah. Can you imagine getting *that* mission?

Cherubim and Seraphim

We don't know very much about these awesome beings, but they too are angels. Interestingly, after Adam and Eve had been ejected from the Garden of Eden for eating the forbidden fruit, God placed cherubim and a flaming sword outside the garden to guard the way to the tree of life.

We read about the seraphim in Ezekiel 1:5, and 21:14. These seem to be angels directly linked to the worship of God. We also encounter them in Isaiah 6:1-3, where it says,

> In the year that King Uzziah died, I saw the Lord seated on a throne, high and exalted, and the train of his robe filled the temple. Above

him were seraphs, each with six wings: With two wings they covered their faces, with two they covered their feet, and with two they were flying. And they were calling to one another: 'Holy, holy, holy is the LORD Almighty; the whole earth is full of his glory.' (NIV)

Now, as you are reading these descriptions of God's mighty angels, you might be thinking to yourself, "Okay. Fine. But what does all this actually have to do with me and my life?"

Actually, more than you might imagine.

Takeaway Truths about Angels

Sometimes angels reveal God's purposes.

You may remember that angels were dispatched to Abraham, to reveal to him the judgment that was about to fall on the cities of the plain. And in the New Testament, I already mentioned how an angel was sent to Zechariah to tell him he would be the father of John the Baptist, and also to Mary and Joseph, declaring God's purposes and giving them special instructions.

The fact is, angels have come to help bring us to salvation, and sometimes give us guidance. The book of Acts tells the fascinating story of when an angel appeared to Cornelius, a Roman centurion. At the time, Cornelius didn't know the Lord, but seemed wide open to things of the Lord. In that instance, the angel revealed to this Roman officer that he needed to meet Simon Peter, who would give to him the gospel.

Have you ever read that story and asked yourself, "Why didn't the angel do that himself? Why didn't this very knowledgeable and ultra-competent envoy from heaven just straight out tell him? Why didn't he give Cornelius the gospel, instead of linking him up with a Christian who was miles away?

Why? Because the primary mission of angels is not to preach the gospel. That is our job. They will help us do it, and they might even guide us in our efforts to do it. But God chooses primarily to reach people through people.

Now if I were God, I don't think I would do it that way. It would seem more efficient to me to just use angels. Angels would always command attention, would always get their facts straight, and wouldn't get distracted or beat around the bush.

But I'm not God (you can be thankful for that), and for whatever reason, He has made a different choice. He reaches people through people, with angels working behind the scenes. In this story, the angel was there to direct Cornelius to go to Peter, so he could hear the gospel.

Another example of angelic direction is in Acts 8 when an angel came to Philip and said, "Go to the desert." And when Philip obeyed and went to that designated place in the wilderness, he came across the path of an Ethiopian official in a chariot who had come all the way to Jerusalem seeking knowledge of God and was now on his way home. And after Philip presented the gospel to him, the man came to faith in Christ.

In the Lion's Den

Daniel was a senior advisor to King Darius, the Mede. He had been advising the kings of Babylon and Medo-Persia for many years, and with great wisdom and integrity. Abundantly blessed by God and in high favor with the king, Daniel also had some enemies, jealous and envious of his success.

Politics never changes very much, does it? The first thing these enemies of Daniel tried to do was to dig up a little dirt on his life so that they could discredit him and undermine him. So they had a meeting, and started looking for ways to bring Daniel down. What were his inconsistencies? What were his weak spots and vulnerabilities? They turned loose the best dirt-diggers, private detectives, and tabloid reporters in the kingdom.

And they came up with *nothing*. A big zero. This was a man of true integrity, without any hidden skeletons in his closet.

Finally they decided, "If we're going to bring this guy down, there's only one way to do it. It has to be concerning him and his God." They concluded this because they knew Daniel had a rock-solid habit of praying three times a day. It was no secret! He would get down on his knees, open up the shutters of his house, and call on the Lord.

They said, "Let's get a law passed that says no one can pray to any god except the king, and if you violate this law you are thrown into a den of lions. It has to work! Because we all know Daniel's going to keep right on praying."

The king, untroubled by anything approaching humility, thought it was a great idea, and signed it into law. In doing so, however, he had no idea he was signing his friend Daniel's death warrant.

So Daniel heard the message: Anybody who prays to any god beside the king will be fed to the lions. And he said, "Really. That's interesting. Now, if you'll excuse me, it's time to go pray."

He prayed to the Lord just as they knew he would, and so he was arrested and sentenced to be executed. There was no way out of this situation apart from God.

Let's pick up the story in Daniel chapter 6.

> So the king gave the command, and they brought Daniel and cast him into the den of lions. But the king spoke, saying to Daniel, "Your God, whom you serve continually, He will deliver you." Then a stone was brought and laid on the mouth of the den, and the king sealed it with his own signet ring and with the signets of his lords, that the purpose concerning Daniel might not be changed.

> Now the king went to his palace and spent the night fasting; and no musicians were brought before him. Also his sleep went from him. Then the king arose very early in the morning and went in haste to the den of lions. And when he came to the den, he cried out with a lamenting voice to Daniel. The king spoke, saying to Daniel, "Daniel, servant of the living God, has your God, whom you serve continually, been able to deliver you from the lions?"

> Then Daniel said to the king, "O king, live forever! My God sent His angel and shut the lions' mouths, so that they have not hurt me, because I was found innocent before Him; and also, O king, I have done no wrong before you." (vv. 16-23)

I'm thinking that Daniel—in a den full of hungry lions—had a good night's sleep. The king, however, with all his musicians and luxury and comfort hadn't been able to sleep at all. Better to be in a lion's den with Jesus than anywhere else without Him! Better to be in the valley of the shadow of death with Christ walking next to me than in the finest home with all of the money this world has to offer. I would rather be anywhere with the Lord than anywhere else without Him.

Maybe you find yourself in something like a lion's den right now. You're surrounded by hostile people, find yourself up against overwhelming odds, or you're walking through a time of great difficulty. Yet the Lord is with you in your dark, confined space, as surely as He was with Daniel. And His angels will protect you until it's time for you to head home to heaven.

When Daniel got that sentence of "death by lions," he probably thought to himself, "What's the worst that could happen? If I get torn apart by lions, I go to heaven to be with my Lord. If I live, I continue to serve the Lord."

The words of David in Psalm 31:14-15 may have very well come to Daniel's mind in that moment:

> But as for me, I trust in you, O LORD;
> I say, "You are my God."
> My times are in your hands.

As it turned out, it wasn't Daniel's time just yet. So the Lord sent His angel to shut the lions' mouths.

Sometimes animals have more sense than people. Those lions probably took one look at the angel and said, "We're not messing with him. Better to skip this meal."

Balaam

I'm reminded of the story of Balaam and his donkey in Numbers chapter 22. Apparently Balaam was a prophet for hire, and the King of Moab had a big job for him. The Moabite ruler wanted Balaam to curse the Israelites as they were passing through the wilderness on their way to the Promised Land.

But the Lord spoke to Balaam and said, "Don't you dare curse those people. They belong to Me." But Balaam was determined to get the money, and was soon on his way, riding on his donkey in the wrong direction to do the wrong thing. That's where we'll pick up the story:

Balaam got up in the morning, saddled his donkey, and went off with the noblemen from Moab. As he was going, though, God's anger flared. The angel of GOD stood in the road to block his way. Balaam was riding his donkey, accompanied by his two servants. When the donkey saw the angel blocking the road and brandishing a sword, she veered off the road into the ditch. Balaam beat the donkey and got her back on the road.

But as they were going through a vineyard, with a fence on either side, the donkey again saw GOD's angel blocking the way and veered into the fence, crushing Balaam's foot against the fence. Balaam hit her again.

GOD's angel blocked the way yet again—a very narrow passage this time; there was no getting through on the right or left. Seeing the angel, Balaam's donkey sat down under him. Balaam lost his temper; he beat the donkey with his stick.

Then GOD gave speech to the donkey. She said to Balaam: "What have I ever done to you that you have beat me these three times?"

Balaam said, "Because you've been playing games with me! If I had a sword I would have killed you by now."

The donkey said to Balaam, "Am I not your trusty donkey on whom you've ridden for years right up until now? Have I ever done anything like this to you before? Have I?"

He said, "No."

Then GOD helped Balaam see what was going on: He saw GOD's angel blocking the way, brandishing a sword. Balaam fell to the ground, his face in the dirt. (Numbers 22:21-31, THE MESSAGE)

Yes there are angels involved in our lives. And sometimes they may stop us from doing the wrong thing or guide us to do the right thing.

I welcome that. I'll take all the help I can get to please the Lord and do the right thing.

Do we have guardian angels? We may. We are told by Jesus that we should not look down on the little ones, meaning the children. He said, "For I tell you their angels in heaven always see the face of My Father in heaven" (Matthew 18:10, NIV). So it may be that at least children have guardian angels. And I'm sure we all know some children who *need* guardian angels, because they're always getting into trouble. In fact, they may have worn out a few angels along the way.

But believers aren't always protected from death and injury are we? What about the times when the lion's mouth isn't closed? What about when you don't narrowly miss that brush with death? What about when death takes you unexpectedly? Does that mean the angels missed their opportunity, or were asleep on the job?

No, it means they have another mission now.

Angels do not determine the time when I am born, nor do they determine the time when I'm going to die. That is up to God. Up until the time of our passing, the role of the angel is guide, to protect, or possibly redirect us. But when the time has come for us to enter into eternity, the role of the angel is to give us an escort into the presence of God.

Escorting Us to Heaven

In Jesus' story of Lazarus and the rich man in Luke 16, we're told how a poor beggar passes out of this life and enters heaven. Jesus said: "The time came when the beggar died and the angels carried him to Abraham's side" (v. 22, NIV).

Death knocks at every door, and is no respecter of persons.

Do you have that hope? Do you know for certain that you will go to heaven when you die? Prior to leaving on a recent trip, I was called to visit with a man who had terminal cancer. I had been told he might not make it another week. I had actually thought about visiting with him after I got back from my trip, but decided I'd better get out there before I left, even though I felt under some time pressure.

So I went to see him. I could tell he was failing physically, yet he remained alert and aware, and we talked at length. There was no question of hiding his condition from him. In fact, he told me himself, "I don't have much longer." So I talked to him about heaven. He had already placed his faith in Jesus, but I wanted to be sure that he was ready.

Finally I said, "Would you like to pray with me right now?" He said "yes", and we prayed. He prayed earnestly and with great passion. And after we were done praying, I comforted him with the promises of God. Finally I said, "I will come back and see you Saturday." But then I got the call late Friday night that he had died.

He took his last breath, and may very well have seen God's majestic, beautiful angels arriving to escort him into the presence of God.

And he was ready.

Are you?

Chapter Nine
THE DARK SIDE

How you are fallen from heaven, O Lucifer, son of the morning!
How you are cut down to the ground–
mighty though you were against the nations of the world.
—Isaiah 14:12, TLB

Where did demons come from?

Short answer: Demons are fallen angels.

As hard as it may be to conceive or believe, there was a rebellion in the angelic world, with many of the angels turning against God and becoming evil. The book of Jude speaks of "angels who did not keep their positions of authority but abandoned their own home" (Jude 6, NIV).

A high-ranking angel named Lucifer led this rebellion of one-third of the angels against God. There are multiple references to this in the Bible. We read of "Beelzebub and his demons" in Matthew 12:24, "the devil and his angels" in Matthew 12:41, and "the dragon and his angels" in Revelation 12:7. Jesus said that hell itself was prepared for the devil and his angels" (Matthew 25:41).

So what is the objective of a demon? What has a demon come to do? Their objectives seem to be two-fold: to seek to hinder the purposes of God, and to extend the power of Satan.

When we say, "I was tempted by the devil the other day," chances are it wasn't the devil himself.

We need to understand that the devil is not God's equal. Though he is a powerful spirit being, Satan's power is nowhere near being the equal of God, which means he can only be in one place at one time. God, however, is *omnipresent*, meaning He is everywhere at once. When you and I are tempted, then, it's probably the activity of one of his demons, doing his dirty work for him.

The apostle Paul spoke about his heart's desire to visit with the church in Thessalonica, but told them, "Therefore we wanted to come to you—even I, Paul, time and again—but Satan hindered us" (1 Thessalonians 2:18). To another group of believers, he spoke of a physical affliction, which he described as a "thorn in the flesh." He went on to say that it was "a messenger from Satan to torment me" (2 Corinthians 12:7, NLT). Through these and many other passages we note that there is an army of demons who will oppose us as we seek to do the work of God.

Why is There a Devil?

As I mentioned in the last chapter, many of us visualize the devil more as a cartoonish caricature rather than a living, powerful, spirit being. As a result, we may not take him as seriously as we ought to.

C. S. Lewis gave this insightful statement about the devil and his demons: "There are two equal and opposite errors into which our race can fall about the devils. One is to disbelieve in their existence. The other is to believe, and to feel an excessive and unhealthy interest in them. They themselves are equally pleased by both errors, and hail a materialist or a magician with the same delight."[48]

It's true; the devil is perfectly content if we don't believe in him. He may even be thinking, "Hey, this is great. I will manipulate your life, and you don't even believe I'm there. That's a good deal for me." Or out on the other extreme, you can have an unhealthy interest in him and demonic powers. There are some people who see demons behind every rock, and everything is about the devil all the time. That's just as unhealthy as the first error.

The truth is, we need a balanced, biblical view of who Satan is. Why?

Because, frankly, he loves the attention. The devil is the ultimate egotist.

But we ask the question, where did the devil come from? What are his tactics? What are his strengths? What are his weaknesses? What can he do? What can't he do? Let's seek to answer some of those questions from Scripture.

Where Did the Devil Come From?

How could a God of love create someone as horrible as the devil?

The very question itself sounds like an accusation, obviously implying it was a bad decision on the part of God.

But God did not create the devil as we know him today.

The Lord created a spirit being, a mighty angel known as Lucifer, or, "son of the morning." Lucifer, however, exercised the free will God had given him and rebelled against his creator. In so doing, he chose to be God's adversary, and became Satan. The devil, then, was not created by God. The devil became what he is by his own volition.

On the other hand, God certainly allowed it.

When did this happen? We can't know for sure, but in Genesis 1:31 we read that "God saw everything that He had made, and behold it was good." By the time we get to Genesis 3, we encounter the serpent, who is tempting Eve. Something must have happened, then, between Genesis 1 and 3 that led to this vast angelic rebellion.

But it didn't start that way.

Lucifer was once a high ranking angel. A radiant, beautiful being. In the book of Ezekiel, we have a fascinating description of Lucifer's fall.

> You were the model of perfection, full of wisdom and perfect in beauty. You were in Eden, the garden of God; every precious stone adorned you: ruby, topaz and emerald, chrysolite, onyx and jasper, sapphire, turquoise and beryl. Your settings and mountings were made of gold; on the day you were created they were prepared. You were anointed as a guardian cherub, for so I ordained you. You were on the holy mount of God; you walked among the fiery stones. You were blameless in your ways from the day you were created till wickedness was found in you. Through your widespread trade you were

filled with violence, and you sinned. So I drove you in disgrace from the mount of God, and I expelled you, O guardian cherub, from among the fiery stones. Your heart became proud on account of your beauty, and you corrupted your wisdom because of your splendor. So I threw you to the earth; I made a spectacle of you before kings. By your many sins and dishonest trade you have desecrated your sanctuaries. So I made a fire come out from you, and it consumed you, and I reduced you to ashes on the ground in the sight of all who were watching. All the nations who knew you are appalled at you; you have come to a horrible end and will be no more. (Ezekiel 28:12-19, NIV)

Have you ever seen a really beautiful girl or handsome guy who *knows* how attractive they are? And everything they do sort of draws attention to themselves. They've never met a mirror they didn't like, and the world just seems to revolve around them. Every conversation ultimately ends up being about them.

That is what Lucifer was like. He was this magnificent spirit being who was clearly a wonder to behold. And that very beauty became his downfall, as he allowed his perfection to become the cause of his corruption. Lucifer, you see, wasn't satisfied with worshipping God. He wanted a piece of the action. He wanted to be worshipped himself, and this "guardian cherub," once an exquisite angel of God, lost his former exalted position in heaven.

Lucifer became Satan when he fell to the earth. In Isaiah 14 we read:

How you are fallen from heaven,
O Lucifer, son of the morning!
How you are cut down to the ground,
You who weakened the nations!
For you have said in your heart:
'I will ascend into heaven,
I will exalt my throne above the stars of God;
I will also sit on the mount of the congregation
On the farthest sides of the north;
I will ascend above the heights of the clouds,
I will be like the Most High.'
Yet you shall be brought down to Sheol,
To the lowest depths of the Pit.
(vv. 12-15)

Jesus says, "I saw Satan fall as lightning from heaven" (Luke 10:18). And as we have noted, when Satan fell he did not fall alone, but took one third of the angels with him.[49]

That's the bad news. The good news is that two thirds of the angels are still with us. We have more angels than he has! But even more importantly, we have the Lord Jesus Christ on our side.

Even though he has fallen, however, Satan still has access to heaven. How do we know this? Because we read in the book of Job how the angels came to present themselves before the Lord, and Satan was among them. God directed His remarks to the devil himself.

"Where have you come from?" the LORD asked Satan.
And Satan answered the LORD, "I have been going back and forth across the earth, watching everything that's going on."
(Job 2:2, NLT)

That is just so creepy isn't it? He is watching everything, checking things out, and his intent toward mankind in general and Christians in particular is all evil all the time.

The Bible describes the devil as a roaring lion seeking whom he may devour.[50] He's like a hungry beast of prey looking for his next meal—and ready to pounce.

Have you seen some of those wildlife TV shows where they film a pride of lions checking out a herd of antelope? The big cats are just hanging out in the sunshine, soaking up the rays, watching the antelope in the distance and kind of sizing them up.

You can almost read their thoughts. "Let's see, which one am I going to eat today?" Inevitably, there's an antelope that's a little slow, and falls behind the rest of the herd. He has V-I-C-T-I-M written all over him. And the lion says to himself, "That looks like lunch to me, because it's a hot day and I really don't want to work too hard." Suddenly, he lunges, catches up to the dawdling antelope and drags it down.

It's an analogy of the way the devil and his demons watch human beings. (Remember his words? "I have been going back and forth across the earth, watching everything that's going on.") He watches. He waits.

He looks for weakness. He probes vulnerabilities. He strategizes on the best way to bring someone down. That is his basic agenda.

And by the way, he's at it 24/7. He never takes a vacation. Don't you wish he did? Wouldn't it be great if I could announce to you, "Guess what I just found out? Satan is taking August off every year. We can have August devil-free."

But no. Our adversary the devil doesn't take a month off—or a week, or a day, or an hour. He is always busy with his well-organized network of demon powers, helping him to accomplish his purposes.

What is the devil's purpose? We could cite any number of things, but here is the end-game, as summarized by Jesus Himself the thief's purpose is to steal and kill and destroy.[51]

Satan may come with some enticing temptation—something that dazzles you or thrills you or has an element of temporary enjoyment in the beginning. But the end game, the ultimate result, is to steal, kill, and destroy.

Names of the Evil One

When Jesus was casting demons out of people, the Pharisees said He did it by the power of *Beelzebub*, the prince of the demons. The name Beelzebub meant "lord of the flies," and the Jews later changed it to the "lord of the dunghill." So that is what Satan is the lord of. The dunghill.

He is also identified as the *prince of this world*. Jesus said, "Now is the time for judgment on this world; now the prince of this world will be driven out. But I, when I am lifted up from the earth, will draw all men to myself" (John 12:31-32, NIV).

Prince of this world? Isn't that a little surprising, hearing Jesus give Satan that title? No, that is exactly what Satan is at this present time. When Jesus was in the wilderness, being tempted by the devil, the evil one showed Him all the kingdoms of the world in a moment of time and said, "All this authority I will give You, and their glory; for this has been delivered to me, and I give it to whomever I wish. Therefore, if You will worship before me, all will be Yours" (Luke 4:6-7).

Effectively, the enemy was saying, "Jesus, I know why You have come. You have come to purchase back that which was lost in the Garden of Eden. But I'm going to make You an offer You cannot refuse. I will give You what You want. Right now! It is all Yours, if you will give me the momentary satisfaction of worship. I want You to worship me."

Of course Jesus resisted that temptation. But it highlights an interesting point. When Satan claimed authority over the kingdoms of the world, *Jesus did not refute this*. Why? Because it is true…for now.

Until Jesus returns to earth as King of kings and Lord of lords, Satan is the *prince of the power of the air*. He is also identified as the god of this world. So he is the one that controls so much of our culture today.

Have you ever wondered why things are as dark as they are? It's really no great mystery, because there is an evil mastermind behind it all. We are talking about a spirit power that infiltrates culture, government, the entertainment world, religious institutions, and the lives of men and women. Day after day, he continues to pull people down with him into temptation, sin, corruption, and death.

Ah, but the devil is clever. If someone isn't attracted by one of his lures he says, "Okay, so you're not into that particular bait. No problem. I've got lots more where that came from."

If the "prince of darkness" image proves to be a turnoff, he also has the ability to mimic some of his former beauty, and can come to us as "an angel of light."[52]

So when a person says, "I'm not into all of that darkness and immorality. I want to learn spirituality. I want to be a religious person."

The devil says, "Really? I've got that covered, too. Check out my new age mysticism. Check out all the tolerant, multi-cultural beliefs I can offer you. I can do a customized package for you, with a little of this and a little of that. All roads lead to God, right?"

No, not right The devil lies about this and a lot of other things as well. Satan is also called "the father of lies." In John 8:44 (NIV), Jesus said,

> You belong to your father, the devil, and you want to carry out your father's desire. He was a murderer from the beginning, not holding

to the truth, for there is no truth in him. When he lies, he speaks his native language, for he is a liar and the father of lies.

Sometimes the devil can just outright lie and a person will immediately swallow the falsehood. He will say to someone, "Right isn't actually right. In fact it is wrong that is right." And the individual will respond, "Oh really? That's interesting. Didn't know that. Okay, I believe it." Other people are a little more discerning, so he will candy-coat his lie with enough truth to make it appealing.

How long has he been employing that technique? Only since the beginning of time!

The First Big Lie

Right from the get-go, Satan has employed his tactic of mixing just a little bit of truth with a deadly dose of outright falsehood. It worked so well in the Garden of Eden that he's been using it ever since.

> Now the serpent was more cunning than any beast of the field which the LORD God had made. And he said to the woman, "Has God indeed said, 'You shall not eat of every tree of the garden'?"
>
> And the woman said to the serpent, "We may eat the fruit of the trees of the garden; but of the fruit of the tree which is in the midst of the garden, God has said, 'You shall not eat it, nor shall you touch it, lest you die.'"
>
> Then the serpent said to the woman, "You will not surely die. For God knows that in the day you eat of it your eyes will be opened, and you will be like God, knowing good and evil."
>
> So when the woman saw that the tree was good for food, that it was pleasant to the eyes, and a tree desirable to make one wise, she took of its fruit and ate. She also gave to her husband with her, and he ate. Then the eyes of both of them were opened, and they knew that they were naked; and they sewed fig leaves together and made themselves coverings. (Genesis 3:1-7)

Right off the bat we can see where things began to go wrong.

Eve was in the wrong place at the wrong time listening to the wrong voice. Why in the world was she hanging around *the one place God told her to avoid?* God had clearly said to stay away from a particular fruit on a particular tree, so out of all the lush, beautiful trees in the garden (and who knows how vast it was), she decided to shade herself under that particular tree.

And guess who was waiting for her there.

It's like telling a little child, "Whatever you do, don't open that cookie jar." You know very well what that child will eventually do. And we are exactly the same way.

Then she listened to the wrong voice. She could have had all the conversation she wanted with God Himself, or her husband, Adam. But she chose to listen to a snake instead.

Oddly enough, I was something of a snake fanatic as a child. I really don't know why, but I loved snakes in those days, and collected all kinds of them. I had corn snakes and gopher snakes and king snakes and even boas. I thought constantly about snakes, read books about snakes, and talked about snakes. (Yes, I know. I had a strange childhood.) I wanted to grow up to become a herpetologist one day, someone who studies reptiles.

So I kept cages stacked on cages with all of these snakes in them.

My mom, however, hated snakes.

One day she was in the house and saw that one of my snakes had escaped, and was slithering across the front room floor. Since it seemed to be heading for the sliding glass patio door, she simply slid the door open and let it slide out of the house to freedom.

"Aw, Mom!" I said later. "That was my best snake!"

Why she put up with all those snakes in the house, I have no idea.

One time I told her that I wanted a particular kind of snake that was at a nearby pet shop. So we got in our baby blue Ford Starliner and went to the shop to check out this new creepy crawler.

I bought the snake and put him in my little terrarium in the trunk, and we drove home. When we opened the trunk, however, my new pet was AWOL. He had somehow escaped into the car.

My mom said, "I am never driving that car again."

Nevertheless, she had to drive it a couple of weeks later, knowing that the snake might still be in there…somewhere. She was very reluctant, but reassured herself by reasoning that the snake had probably escaped by that time.

Pulling up to a red light at an intersection, she suddenly felt a cold coil drop onto her ankle. The snake! She threw open the door, jumped out and ran into the intersection, screaming, "There's a snake in the car!"

A police officer happened to be nearby, and came over to her.

"Ma'am, what is wrong?"

"There's a snake in the car!"

He went over to the car to look, and spotted what had given her such a fright. One of those hoses under the dashboard had come loose and fallen on her ankle.

She said, "I am never driving this car again!" And this time she meant it. She gave me the car, and it all worked out pretty well for me! (I wish I had held on to that car, as it really is a collectable now.)

Snakes are escape artists, and very clever. They seem to be able to get out of (or into) the tightest of places. In other words, if you're living in an area where there are snakes, it pays to be cautious.

Something else I've learned about snakes. Did you know that the venom of a baby rattlesnake is more potent than that of an adult? Have you ever seen a baby rattler? They're actually kind of a cute, because everything is miniaturized, right down to the little rattle.

But make no mistake about it, the bite of a baby rattler will kill you.

In the same way we will say, "This is just a little baby sin. Hardly worth worrying about. It's just a small compromise. It really isn't a big deal. I can do this little thing one time, and it won't lead to anything else. I can handle this."

Watch out! An unguarded strength is a double weakness. Don't ever say, "I will never fall in this one area." Don't you believe it or let down your guard! Because that is the very area where Satan may trip you up.

The Bible says, "Pride goes before destruction, and a haughty spirit before a fall" (Proverbs 16:18).

Frankly, you don't know what you might be capable of in a given set of circumstances. You need to keep your guard up at all times, because it is in these little deals we make with the devil—the small, seemingly harmless compromises—that lead to bigger and more devastating things later.

Satan is smart. Don't underestimate him. Stay alert (as the New Testament says again and again) and watch your thoughts.

Please note, however, that it is *not* a sin to be tempted. As Martin Luther observed, "You can't stop a bird from flying over your head, but you can stop it from making a nest in your hair."

In other words, the sin is not in the bait, it's in the bite. Just because bait was dangled before you doesn't mean you have done anything wrong. In fact, if someone tells me that they're never tempted, I have to wonder what's wrong with them. The very fact that you *do* struggle with temptation from time to time is an indication that you're moving forward spiritually, and that the devil would like to bring you down. So if you have faced temptation and attack lately, it may very well mean you're doing something *right*.

Packaging Sin

Satan certainly understands humankind after all these years and all his experience of dealing with us. As a result, he knows how to make things look very, very appealing. In the Genesis passage we read earlier, it says, "The woman saw that the tree was good for food, that it was pleasant to the eyes, and a tree desirable to make one wise…" (Genesis 31:6).

In other words, it had a lot of eye appeal.

That fruit looked good.

By the way, the Bible never says that it was an *apple*. Just speaking personally, an apple wouldn't have tempted me at all. Now a nice ripe peach or nectarine maybe…. But I suggest it was a piece of fruit like you have never seen before. There was something unbelievably attractive about it. Maybe it glowed or pulsated, and Eve was drawn to it. *Wow, what's this?*

When she approached the tree, Satan was ready, and had his lines down cold. He knew what he would say to her. If she ate of this fruit, she would become a goddess, and know as much as heaven knew. In fact, wasn't it just a little bit strange that God was holding out on her, keeping something back from her? If God really loved her, He would let her have this marvelous fruit, wouldn't He?

Satan will say the same thing to us. "If God really loved you, He would let you do whatever you want to do. If God really loved you, He would allow you to chase after whatever passion interests you. If God really loved you He wouldn't have allowed this to happen to you." That is what he was doing with Eve. He was challenging the Word of God, and he was challenging God's love for her.

It worked, and Eve fell.

We, however, must resist.

The apostle James says, "But resist the devil and you'll find he'll run away from you" (Proverbs 16:18). The temptations will come, they will never stop coming, and they will come in unexpected ways at unexpected times, as Satan adapts his strategies.

We simply have to be ready. We have to be able to say of our adversary, "for we are not ignorant of his devices" (2 Corinthians 2:11).

Imagine you're playing tennis with someone, and you are rallying for serve. So you're hitting the ball back and forth across the net, and as you are, you're taking note of your opponent's game—sizing him up. You might say to yourself, "Ah-hah. He's not very strong off his backhand." Or you might notice that he's not very effective when he has to rush the net. So after awhile, you develop a strategy of how to play him, and how to take advantage of his weak areas. Then you'll start scoring some points, because the object is to defeat your opponent and win the game.

It's the same way with the devil. He will say, "Oh, I see he's strong in this area. I'll try something else." Or, "She seems to lack confidence in that area—I'll go after it harder."

That's why we've always got to keep our guard up. The devil never takes a day off, and neither can we take a day off from spiritual warfare. The Christian life is not a playground, it's a battleground, and we are either winning or losing, advancing or retreating.

And the stakes are very, very high.

So let's keep our eyes open and our minds protected. Because the Bible tells us that we are to bring every thought into the captivity of the obedience of Jesus Christ.[53]

Strategies from Hell

So Satan attacks us, and here is how his strategy works.

First he will come as the enticer. Then he will come as the accuser.

As the enticer, or the tempter, he will whisper in your ear, "You deserve a break today. You work so hard, and you're such a committed Christian. You're doing a great job and have been really strong. In fact, you are so strong it really wouldn't even matter if you compromised in this little area, or gave in a little over here. What difference could it make? Anyway, it will be fun (and it's about time you had a little fun, don't you think?) Besides, it's no big deal. Everyone else is doing it. Go ahead! I won't tell anyone if you won't. Come on, just this once!"

So you say, "Well, okay…I'll do it." And you do.

Almost immediately, the devil comes back to you and says, "You pathetic hypocrite. Look at you! You call yourself a follower of Jesus after what you just did? Don't even think about showing your face in church again! And don't open that Bible. Oh man, that would be so hypocritical for you to open the Bible. And don't pray. Don't you dare call out to God. That would be so wrong."

And sometimes we listen to this stuff, and fall right into his strategy. Yes, he is certainly the tempter. But he is equally adept as an *accuser*. The Bible says he is "the accuser of our brothers, who accuses them before our God day and night" (Revelation 12:10, NIV).

So what about this thing called guilt?

When you sin, you will feel guilt. And that is a good thing. Guilt simply means your conscience is working. The time to be concerned is when you *don't* feel guilt. The time to be concerned is when you can sin against God again and again and feel no remorse or sense of wrongdoing. The Bible says in the book of Hebrews, "Whom the Lord loves He chastens" (Hebrews 12:6). That means that when you, as a son or daughter of God, go astray, the Holy Spirit will convict you of your sin and say, "That is wrong." He will call you on it, because He loves you. "Don't do that. That is wrong. Stop it now." Just like a father or mother would reprove a child.

When my sons were growing up, it was my responsibility to correct my own children, not someone else's children—though I would like to have done that at times. You see a child talking back to his mom and just being naughty, and you feel like saying, "Let me step in here." But no, you can't do that. That's not your privilege. But it is your responsibility to bring correction to your own sons and daughters.

In the same way God, disciplines His own children. But if you are without discipline, if you can do things that you know are wrong and don't feel any remorse, I think you have to wonder whether you are truly a child of God. But if you feel busted the moment you cross the line and come under the conviction of the Spirit, I say hallelujah. Your conscience is working. And the Spirit is working in your life, correcting you and changing you from the inside out.

Guilt, however, is meant to lead me to a correct response. And when I have responded appropriately, turning from that sin and seeking the Lord's forgiveness, the guilt can go away, because it has served its purpose.

It's very important that we learn the difference between the legitimate conviction of the Holy Spirit, and the devil's accusations, meant to damage or destroy us. The devil will use your sins in a hateful way to drive you away from the cross. The Holy Spirit will convict you of your sins in a loving way to bring you to the cross.

Let me put it another way. Satan will always try to keep you from the cross. The Holy Spirit will always bring you to the cross.

Here's how it works. You have sinned, and you know you have sinned. You say to yourself, *Oh no. I can't believe I just did that*. The devil says to you, "Run. Go. Get away. Get by yourself and sulk or maybe despair a little. But don't go to God." The Holy Spirit, however, says, "Yes, you have sinned. But repent now. Get back into fellowship with the God who loves you." So right there on the spot you say, "Lord, I'm sorry. I know that I was wrong. I repent of that sin. I ask You to forgive me right now. In Jesus' name."

And then, after you have asked God for forgiveness, you don't need to keep going over and over it again. You don't need to keep berating yourself or kicking yourself or calling yourself names.

Why? Because your God has a big eraser. And if He has used it in your life, then be thankful! Your sin is not only forgiven, but it is forgotten. We know that, because God has said, "Their sins and their iniquities will I remember no more" (Hebrews 8:12, KJV).

The devil, however, will try to push you into despair over your failures. He will try to use your sins to drive a wedge between you and your heavenly Father.

Don't listen to him.

Not then, not ever.

As I pointed out, he is a liar and the father of lies.

When you think about it, both Judas and Peter betrayed the Lord on the same night—Judas for thirty pieces of silver, and Peter before the servant of the high priest. I believe that if Judas had wanted it, Jesus would have forgiven him and restored him.

In the Garden of Gethsemane when Judas came to identify Jesus as the one the authorities were looking for, he did so by kissing Him.

Jesus said to him, "Why have you come?"[54]

Jesus was God. He knew all things, and knew very well what Judas was doing. I believe in that moment, however, Jesus was offering His disciple a final chance for repentance and forgiveness.

Judas, however, plunged on ahead with his evil plan, and betrayed

Jesus. Sometime later, however, the enormity of what he had done dawned on him. And although he was filled with regret, we never read that he actually repented or turned back to the Lord. Instead, he listened to the voice of the one who "kills, steals, and destroys"…and went out and hung himself.[55]

For his part, at a crucial moment, Simon Peter had denied even knowing the Lord—not once, not twice, but three times. Scripture says he uttered an oath to that effect, which essentially means, "I swear to God I never knew Jesus."

And then the rooster crowed, he made eye contact with the Lord Jesus, and went outside to weep.[56] After that, however, he stayed with his Christian friends, turned back to the Lord, and Jesus forgave and restored him. Judas had listened to the wrong voice, and ended up destroying himself; Peter listened to the right voice, did the right thing, and went on to great kingdom exploits.

We're all going to sin; it's not a matter of *if*, it's a matter of *when*. The Bible tells us very clearly, "If we claim to be without sin, we deceive ourselves and the truth is not in us" (1 John 1:8, NIV).

The question is, what will we do when we sin? Will we listen to the wrong voice and do wrong, destructive things, or will we listen to the right voice, and find healing, hope, and full restoration? The wrong voice, the devil, would drive us from Jesus, from church, from fellowship, from the Word of God, and from everything that could help us. But if we listen to the right voice, the voice of the Holy Spirit, He will direct us back to the Word of God, to church, to our Christian friends, to the Lord in prayer, and to the great joy of an intimate relationship with the living God.

It's our choice.

Let's choose wisely.

Chapter Ten
THE REALITY OF HELL

And death and the grave were thrown into the lake of fire. This is the second death — the lake of fire. And anyone whose name was not found recorded in the Book of Life was thrown into the lake of fire. —Revelation 20:14-15, NLT

Not long ago on a Christian television show, the interviewer asked me why I spoke so much about eternity.

"When I've watched you preach on your TV program or at a crusade," he said, "I've noticed whatever topic you're dealing with, you always come back to eternity."

I'd never really noticed that before. Since my son went to heaven in 2008, I suppose it's truer now than ever.

"So why do you do that?" he asked me. "Why do you always come back to the eternal in your messages?"

After thinking about it for a moment, I answered, "I guess when you get down to it, it's the most important thing there is."

As a pastor I want to teach the Word of God, and help people grow in their faith as followers of Jesus. I want them to learn how to know God's will, resist temptation, build a great marriage, walk in integrity, and all those things we talk about as pastors and teachers. But when it's all said and done, the most important thing to me is intercepting people on their way to hell, and pointing them toward heaven instead.

I want people to change their eternal address.

So that is why I do what I do.

We will talk at length about heaven in the chapters to come. Most people believe in some kind of heaven, and also believe they're going there. Statistics show that for every American who believes he or she is going to hell, there are 120 who believe they'll end up in heaven.

That is a direct contradiction, however, to what Jesus said.

"Enter by the narrow gate; for wide is the gate and broad is the way that leads to destruction, and there are many who go in by it. Because narrow is the gate and difficult is the way which leads to life, and there are few who find it." (Matthew 7:13-14)

No matter how fervently we might wish it otherwise, Jesus teaches that most people today are not headed to heaven. If we believe the Bible we have to accept this simple fact. Most people are actually headed to hell, though none of us likes to hear that.

It's interesting to me that even though many in our culture don't believe in a literal hell, people will use the word to punctuate their sentences.

Someone will say, "All hell just broke loose." Or maybe, "He really gave me hell." Or even, "You go to hell."

That last phrase is used a lot, to insult someone. But at the same time, if someone had a great time somewhere they will say, "Man, we had a hell of a good time together."

I actually had a guy come up to me after a message on a Sunday morning, shake my hand and say, "That was a hell of a speech, Reverend."

I actually laughed. I didn't know what else to do. I supposed in his own way he was trying to compliment me. I said, "Well, I was hoping it was a *heaven* of a speech." But I understood what he was saying.

It's funny how someone will say to another person, "You can go to hell," but at the same time they will say, "I don't believe a place called hell actually exists." I guess it's not quite as effective to say to yell at someone and say, "You can just go to a place that doesn't exist!"

Why do people say, "Go to hell?" Because deep down inside, even if you are a nonbeliever, you *know* there is a hell.

Hell is a real place, but because we are uncomfortable with that idea we will make jokes about it. Did you know that there is an actual town in Michigan called Hell? Can you imagine? It was founded in 1841, by a man named George Reeves, who had discovered a low, swampy place in Southeast Michigan and didn't know what to name it. Someone said to him, "What do you want to call it?" And he replied, "I don't care. Name it Hell, if you want to."

And so they did. Hell, Michigan.

People feel free to joke about the topic of hell. Comedian Woody Allen said, "Hell is the future abode of all people who personally annoy me."[57] Jim Carrey said, "Maybe there is no actual place called hell. Maybe hell is just having to listen to our grandparents breathe through their noses when they are eating sandwiches."[58]

But there is a hell. A real hell. And it's no joke.

The fact of the matter is that Jesus Christ spoke more about hell than all of the other prophets and preachers of the Bible put together. Most of the teaching we have on the topic of hell was given to us by Christ Himself.

That fact surprises some people. They will say, "Really? Wasn't Jesus the very personification of love and mercy and grace? Why would He talk about hell?"

For that very reason! It's precisely because He was and is the personification of love and grace and mercy that He doesn't want any man or woman uniquely made in His image to spend eternity in this place called hell. And Jesus, being God, knows about it because He has seen it with His own eyes. As a result, He carefully, sternly, and repeatedly warns us about its existence.

It has been estimated that of the forty parables that Jesus told, more than half of them dealt with God's eternal judgment and hell. Make no mistake about it; there is a real hell for real people.

J. I. Packer said, "An endless hell can no more be removed from the New Testament than an endless heaven can."[59] It is there.

It's interesting to me how the concept of judgment in the afterlife becomes more or less popular, depending on the time in which we are living. I think belief in hell probably went up after 9/11, because when some great evil takes place, people tend to believe in a place of final retribution. But when things aren't going as badly and the memory of mass murderers fades a little, then a belief in hell actually starts to tail off.

Years ago John Lennon famously sang, "Imagine there is no heaven. It is easy if you try. No hell below us. Above us only sky."

Dear John: We can "imagine" all we want, but it won't change eternal realities. There is a heaven. And there is a hell.

The Second Death

The Bible actually teaches that there are two deaths, one physical, and one spiritual. Furthermore, Jesus warned that we are to fear the second death more than the first! In Revelation 20:14 we read, "Then Death and Hades were cast into the lake of fire. This is the second death." In Revelation 21:8 (NLT), the One who sits on the throne says, "But cowards, unbelievers, the corrupt, murderers, the immoral, those who practice witchcraft, idol worshipers, and all liars—their doom is in the lake that burns with fire and sulfur. This is the second death."

The second death is hell, which is eternal separation from God. One commentator wrote, "Eternity to the godly is a day that has no sunset. Eternity to the wicked is a night that has no sunrise."

The Bible describes hell in different ways.

Hell is pictured like a garbage dump.

One picture we have of hell in the Bible is that of a garbage dump. But not like any garbage dump we have ever seen. I don't know if you have ever taken your own trash to the dump and looked around at all the rubbish and castoff items. You'll see an old refrigerator and a television set and maybe even part of a car sticking out of the garbage. You think how hard people must have worked at one time to obtain those items, and now here they are, moldering in a landfill.

But the dump in New Testament days, also known as Gehenna, was far worse than that. You would not only throw your trash and rubbish there, but it was a place where they could toss in dead bodies as well, and it was constantly smoldering and burning. You can imagine what a horrific place this was.

So Jesus takes the picture of Gehenna, the dump, if you will, and uses it to describe hell.

Hell is pictured like a prison.

One of the clearest pictures Christ gave of hell was that of being incarcerated. He told a parable of a king's servant who was sent to jail for cruel and unforgiving behavior then added this warning, "This is how my heavenly Father will treat each of you unless you forgive your brother from your heart" (Matthew 18:35, NIV).

I don't know if you have ever been to prison. I receive letters on occasion from people in prison who listen to our radio broadcast.

When we were doing a crusade in South Dakota, I had the honor of receiving a special blanket from some Christian Native Americans there. The man who gave me the blanket first heard the gospel on our radio broadcast in prison and came to Christ. Now he is serving the Lord and preaching the gospel. That was an encouraging thing to hear.

In this prison called hell, however, there will be no opportunities to repent or to find release. It will be too late for that.

Hell is pictured like a fire that never stops burning.

The most well-known picture given to us in Scripture is where hell is likened to a fire that never stops burning. That brings us to a story in Luke 16, where Jesus spoke of hell as an unquenchable fire.

The Story of Lazarus and the Beggar

Jesus told many parables or stories to make His points clear, but I don't believe that the account in Luke 16 is a parable. I think it's a true account of real people and real events.

Why do I believe that? Because Jesus uses actual names in the story, and He doesn't do that in His parables. So you might describe this as a behind-the-scenes look into the invisible world. If you have wondered what happens on the other side when believers and nonbelievers pass into eternity, here is a glimpse into those realms provided by Christ Himself.

> There was a certain rich man who was clothed in purple and fine linen and fared sumptuously every day. But there was a certain beggar named Lazarus, full of sores, who was laid at his gate, desiring to be fed with the crumbs which fell from the rich man's table. Moreover the dogs came and licked his sores. So it was that the beggar died, and was carried by the angels to Abraham's bosom. The rich man also died and was buried. And being in torments in Hades, he lifted up his eyes and saw Abraham afar off, and Lazarus in his bosom.
>
> Then he cried and said, 'Father Abraham, have mercy on me, and send Lazarus that he may dip the tip of his finger in water and cool my tongue; for I am tormented in this flame.' But Abraham said, 'Son, remember that in your lifetime you received your good things, and likewise Lazarus evil things; but now he is comforted and you are tormented. And besides all this, between us and you there is a great gulf fixed, so that those who want to pass from here to you cannot, nor can those from there pass to us.'
>
> Then he said, 'I beg you therefore, father, that you would send him to my father's house, for I have five brothers, that he may testify to them, lest they also come to this place of torment.' Abraham said to him, 'They have Moses and the prophets; let them hear them.' And he said, 'No, father Abraham; but if one goes to them from the dead, they will repent.' But he said to him, 'If they do not hear Moses and the prophets, neither will they be persuaded though one rise from the dead.' (Luke 16:19-31)

Jesus mentions the name of the beggar, Lazarus. The wealthy man in the story is described as "a certain rich man."

One man owned everything, yet possessed nothing.

The other owned nothing, but inherited everything.

One went to comfort, the other went to torment.

The believing man, Lazarus, was ushered by the angels into the presence of God, into a place called Paradise.

By the way, prior to the arrival of Jesus and His death and resurrection, when a person would die in faith they went to a place called "Paradise" or to "Abraham's bosom," as the King James Version describes it.

When Jesus was crucified and the man on the cross next to Him came to His senses and asked the Lord for mercy, Jesus said to him, "I assure you, today you will be with me in paradise" (Luke 23:43, NLT).

So that thief who had been crucified next to Jesus went into a place of waiting, a realm of bliss and comfort called Paradise. That was before Jesus had been raised from the dead. But the Bible says that after His death and resurrection, a believer who dies goes straight to heaven and into the presence of God. The apostle Paul told us that to be absent from the body is to be present with the Lord.[60]

One other thing about that thief on the cross. You might describe what happened to him as a deathbed conversion. And I hope this gives a measure of encouragement to you to never stop praying for friends and loved ones who are still outside of Jesus Christ. Time and again, I've heard glorious stories of people who have come to the Lord right before passing into eternity.

Sometimes we know someone who died and we fear they are in hell right now. I've heard people say, "That person is in hell."

The truth is, you and I don't know who is in hell. We're in no position to say. Now I do think we can authoritatively say who is in heaven. If an individual has put their faith in Christ, we can say, "They're with the Lord, now." And the Bible assures us of this. But who are we to say what may or may not have happened to an individual in those final seconds before leaving this life?

I know this: If a person cries out to Jesus in repentance with their last breath or last fading thought, God will forgive them and accept them into heaven. Remember this: No one wants to save a person more than the Lord Jesus Christ.

But what happens if a person truly rejects God's salvation to the very end? We have a picture of that in this story Jesus told in Luke 16.

Tormented

The rich man also died and was buried. And being in torments in Hades, (or hell) he lifted up his eyes and saw Abraham afar off, and

Lazarus in his bosom. (Luke 16:22-23)

The sin of this man was not his wealth; the sin of this man was that he had no time for God. You might say that he was possessed by his possessions. The Bible says he fared sumptuously, and was clothed in purple and fine linen.

In this culture, purple was the color of royalty. Clothing makers would crush a special worm and use the dye to produce this luxurious garment, only worn by the richest of the rich. And this man was clothed in purple and fine linen from head to foot. The account also tells us that this man "fared sumptuously *every day.*" That's another way of saying he had a daily, non-stop banquet going on. He was apparently really into food, and had unlimited resources to eat whatever he wanted.

It was a different story for the beggar lying out by his front gate. His name was Lazarus, and he was weak, covered with sores, and severely impoverished—to the point of starvation. Apparently, he had been living off of the scraps from the rich man's table—when he could get them.

In those days, people didn't eat with a knife and fork. They didn't use utensils at all. They would pick the food up with their hands using bits of bread, and then they would wipe their hands on pieces of bread and throw them on the floor for the dogs to eat.

That was Lazarus's diet. We are also told that he was carried to the rich man's estate and laid at his gate, which would imply that he either disabled or maybe so weak and sick that he couldn't walk.

Surely, the rich man saw Lazarus's situation. He could have invited him to his table, or at the very least, sent a proper meal out to him. But he cared nothing about Lazarus. His mind was filled with "looking out after number one," and having his non-stop feast of pleasing himself.

But then death came.

And death is the great equalizer.

When the rich man died, it probably made all the papers. It was a big deal for a few hours. Then the poor man died, and it didn't even make a ripple on earth. No one really cared about him. But God did! And Lazarus was ushered into Paradise by angels.

It was now time for the rich man to face the repercussions of life that had no room for God. And he was going to find out that it wasn't so glamorous on the other side.

Malcolm Forbes, one of the world's wealthiest men, said shortly before his death, "The thing I dread most about death is that I know I will not be as comfortable in the next life as I was in this one."[61]

I have no idea where Mr. Forbes was at spiritually, but for the sake of a point, if you don't know God, you can be sure it won't be as comfortable on the other side.

What Do We Learn from This Story?

#1 People in hell suffer.

The fact that this man spoke of torment indicates that suffering is a very real thing in the hereafter. In fact the word "torment" is used four times in the text of this story. People in hell are fully conscious, and they are in pain. It doesn't say that this man went to purgatory. There is no such thing as a place called purgatory. Nor was he reincarnated as a higher or a lower life form. Once you pass from this life you pass into eternity, into either heaven or hell. This man was in hell.

#2 Once you are in hell, you can't cross over to heaven.

Sometimes people will say, "When I stand before God, I've got the gift of gab, and me and the Man Upstairs will sort this out."

But there will be no more sorting out. It will be too late for that; once you are in eternity there is no changing things.

It's different now. While there is life, it is still possible to change things—including your eternal destination! There are no chances after death, but thousands before.

The Bible says, "It is appointed for men to die once, but after this the judgment" (Hebrews 9:27).

Physical death is a separation of the soul from the body, and constitutes a transition from the visible world to the invisible world. For the believer it is entrance into paradise, into the presence of Jesus. For the nonbeliever, it marks his entrance into Hades. Physical death is not the end of existence, but only a change in the state of existence.

#3 When you are in hell, you are conscious and fully aware of where you are.

You are also aware of where you were. In heaven, as we will discuss later, you will still be you. You will still know what you knew on earth, but far more. You will be aware of where you came from, and of where you are. In the same way, in hell you will be cognizant of where you came from and where you are, as this man speaks about his five brothers in Luke 16, verse 28. "I have five brothers," he says, "And someone needs to testify to them so they don't come to this place of torment."

In a way this man was blame-shifting. It's as though he were saying, "Hey, I really didn't know about this. No one warned me!" Abraham, however, corrects him in verse 29: "They have Moses and the prophets. Let them hear them." And the man replies, "No, father Abraham; but if one goes to them from the dead, they will repent" (v. 39).

Really?

Well, one man actually did come back from the dead. His name was Lazarus, too, but it wasn't the same Lazarus in this story. This Lazarus was a personal friend of Jesus, and the Lord raised him from the dead after he'd been in the tomb for four days.

But even though the miracle was verified by many people, it only made the religious leaders of the day more determined than ever to kill Jesus—and Lazarus, too, if they could manage it. And they were speaking this way even though they acknowledged "This man certainly performs many miraculous signs" (John 11:47, NLT).

So here was a dead man who came back to life. But still the Jewish leaders refused to believe.

Even more to the point, Jesus Christ Himself rose again from the dead, and was seen by as many as 500 people at one time.[62] Did everyone believe? No. Really only a small percentage of the people did. So the rich man's argument that "someone coming back from the dead" would cause his brothers to believe just wasn't true.

The Great White Throne

So after death, the nonbeliever goes to a place of torment. But that isn't the end of it. There is still a judgment yet to come, known as the Great White Throne—a terrible final judgment, for nonbelievers only.

> Then I saw a great white throne and Him who sat on it, from whose face the earth and the heaven fled away. And there was found no place for them. And I saw the dead, small and great, standing before God, and books were opened. And another book was opened, which is the Book of Life. And the dead were judged according to their works, by the things which were written in the books. The sea gave up the dead who were in it, and Death and Hades delivered up the dead who were in them. And they were judged, each one according to his works. Then Death and Hades were cast into the lake of fire. This is the second death. And anyone not found written in the Book of Life was cast into the lake of fire. (Revelation 20:11-15)

Who will be at the Great White Throne judgment?

Answer: Everyone who has rejected God's offer of forgiveness through Jesus Christ. Notice that there are no exceptions. Verse 12: "I saw the dead, small and great, standing before God, and the books were opened."

God is no respecter of persons. The fact that a person may have been a king or a queen, an emperor or president, a prime minister or rock star doesn't matter. Everyone standing before that throne is in the same position, and each person has to give an account of his or her life.

Actor Robert De Niro was asked the question, "If there are pearly gates and you stand before God one day, what will you say to Him?" De Niro's response was, "I will say to God, if heaven exists, He has a lot of explaining to do."[63]

No. I don't think so.

At this Great White Throne, everyone will have to give an account of the life they have lived. The big issue in this final judgment however, won't be a *sin* issue as much as it will be a *Son* issue.

The greatest and final question in the last day will be, "What did You do with the offer of salvation in My Son, Jesus Christ?"

The apostle John put it very, very simply: "And this is the testimony: God has given us eternal life, and this life is in his Son. He who has the Son has life; he who does not have the Son of God does not have life" (1 John 5:11-12, NIV).

The fact is, good people don't go to heaven. Forgiven people do. Because apart from the gift of righteousness in Jesus, no one is good enough.

Why is a Person at the Great White Throne Judgment?

They will be there because they did not believe in Jesus, and receive His offer of forgiveness and salvation.

In John 3:18, Jesus said: "He that believes in Me is not condemned; but he that does not believe in Me is condemned already, because he has not believed in the name of the only begotten Son of God."

If the nonbeliever is already condemned, then what is the purpose of the last judgment?

This is a very important question. The purpose of the final confrontation between God and man is to clearly demonstrate to the nonbeliever *why* he is already condemned.

If someone spoke up at that judgment and said, "Wait a second, I never knew about this," their argument would be refuted, because in Revelation 20:12, it says that "the books were opened." What are these books? We don't know for certain, but one of them may be a book of God's law. And everyone who has been exposed to the truth of God's law will be held responsible. As Romans 3:19 says, "so that every mouth may be silenced and the whole world held accountable to God."

I bring this up because some people will say, "I really don't need Jesus Christ. I just live by the Ten Commandments."

No, actually you don't.

Have you ever taken the Lord's name in vain—using it in an

empty, insincere, frivolous way? Have you ever taken anything that didn't belong to you? Have you ever lied? Of course you have. The fact is, if you want to live by the law you're in deep trouble, because the Bible says, "If you offend in one point of the law you are guilty of all of it."

The law was never given to make a man or a woman righteous. The law is a moral mirror that shows us our real state before God—and its intent is to drive us into the open arms of Jesus. The law says, "You are not good enough. You need God's help."

Maybe another book opened at the Great White Throne would be a record of everything you have ever said or done. That's not so hard to believe, because in this high-tech world of ours, you're being recorded by some kind of surveillance camera almost everywhere you go. If you run a red light, you might get your picture taken, and there will be no getting out of that ticket.

If you think that mankind can do this in an increasingly effective way, don't you imagine that the Creator of the uNIVerse might have some pretty tricked out and sophisticated recording equipment?

Actually, you can be sure of it.

The Bible tells us that everything we do, whether good or bad, is recorded, and we will be judged for it:

For God will bring every deed into judgment,
including every secret thing,
whether it is good or evil.
(Ecclesiastes 12:14, NIV)

"But I say to you that for every idle word men may speak,
they will give account of it in the day of judgment."
(Matthew 12:36)

The most important book of all, however, is the Book of Life.

"And anyone not found written in the Book of Life was cast into the lake of fire."

Some people will say, "That's just not right. How could a God of love create a place called hell?"

The truth is, it is *because* He is a God of love that He created a place called hell. There are terrible injustices in this life, and wrongs done that people should never get away with. And though they may escape the long arm of the law, they will never escape the long arm of God.

Justice will be done, and that justice will be final and complete.

Beyond all of that, however, hell was not made for people. Jesus said hell was created for the devil and his angels.[64] It was never God's intention to send a person to hell, and He does everything He can to keep people out of hell.

But in the final analysis, it's our choice.

God has given to you and to me a free will. I have the ability to choose, and God will not violate that. If you want to go to heaven, my friend, you will, if you put your faith in Christ. If you want to go to hell, you will. That is really your choice.

J. I. Packer writes, "Scripture sees hell as self-chosen. Hell appears as God's gesture of respect for human choice. All receive what they actually choose. Either to be with God forever worshipping Him or without God forever worshipping themselves."[65]

C. S. Lewis said, "There are only two kinds of people in the end. Those who say to God, 'Thy will be done' and those to whom God says in the end, 'Thy will be done.' All that are in hell choose it. Without that self-choice there could be no Hell."[66]

Timothy Keller said, "All God does in the end with people is give them what they most want, including freedom from himself. What could be fairer than that?" Indeed, hell is … "the trajectory of a soul, living a self-absorbed, self-centered life, going on and on forever." [67]

In the end, we get what we most truly want.

It's not enjoyable to preach or write about these things. But if you belong to Jesus Christ, I hope that being reminded of these realities will make you want to redouble your efforts to reach people with the gospel. The Bible tells us to "Rescue others by snatching them from the flames of judgment. There are still others to whom you need to show mercy, but be careful that you aren't contaminated by their sins" (Jude 23, NLT).

Sometimes we don't warn people about hell because we don't want to offend them. We're willing to talk about the glories of walking with Christ, and how He gives us peace and joy and purpose, but the person just blows us off, and says, "I don't need that. I'm happy enough as I am."

But there is a warning in the gospel, too.

Yes, there is a heaven to gain, but there is also a hell to avoid.

Just a brief warning, but then the message turns positive again. God poured all of His judgment on Jesus 2,000 years ago at the cross, so you and I would not have to go to a place called hell. And He will forgive you of every wrong you have ever done if you will turn to Him.

And right now would be the best time of all.

Chapter Eleven
LET'S TALK ABOUT HEAVEN

No one's ever seen or heard anything like this, Never so much as imagined anything quite like it– What God has arranged for those who love him.
—1 Corinthians 2:9, The Message

Ever since I was a little boy I have always been a fan of Disney. When I was growing up, of course, Walt Disney himself was still the creative genius behind the whole Disney empire. Like so many in my generation, I was raised watching the Mickey Mouse Club on my black and white TV. (With rabbit ears. Remember those? That was before cable or satellite.)

And then of course, just around the time when color television was introduced, there was the "Wonderful World of Disney" on Sunday nights. Even before that time, I remember when Walt Disney came out before the cameras, unrolled some architectural plans on his desk, and said, "I want to tell you about something we are building now. We call it, *Disneyland*."

Disneyland. As a little kid watching this, it was more like *The Promised Land*. I could hardly wait to get to this place. To me, it seemed like the ultimate escape from the crazy alcoholic home I was raised in, and all the different men living with my mother and coming and going through my life.

Most of all, it was a promise of something better.

Living in Southern California as we did, I made my mom take me to Disneyland for my birthday. To this day, I can remember making a vow as we approached the park and I looked at the Matterhorn in the distance. I said to myself: "Someday, when I become an adult, I'm going to go to Disneyland every single day."

I haven't quite lived up to that vow, though I'm sure I've had more than my share of days at the Magic Kingdom. But why did Disneyland draw me so strongly when I was a child? Because, as I said, it held so much promise.

Disney was a dreamer. He called the people who worked with him "imagineers," as the whole Disney team spent time imaging what could be. He was raised in the Midwest, and didn't have much money. But he always dreamt of a better world—or possibly even of *creating* a better world. You might even say he was trying to create a heaven on earth.

In his Disney biography, author Pat Williams wrote:

I know that Walt Disney felt a longing for heaven. He had that longing when he was a boy in Kansas City peering through the fence at Electric Park, wanting what he couldn't have because he didn't have a dime in his pocket. I believe it was that longing for heaven that drove Walt to build a perfect place where children could ride merry-go-rounds and always catch the brass ring. A place where yesterday and tomorrow were always within walking distance. A place where anyone can be perfectly happy, if only for a day. In Walt's mind, heaven is a beautiful park all shining and clean filled wonderful things to see and do, with a castle rising over it all and a train that goes around it.[68]

Walt Disney isn't really so much different from you and me. We, too, have been pre-wired to want something more in life. The Bible says that we have been born with eternity in our hearts.[69] That is something that is unique to mankind, to men and women made in the image of God.

It's not true of the animal kingdom. I don't think animals sit around and wonder about the meaning of life. Dogs don't. Definitely cats never would. I can't imagine one of my dogs lying in the backyard thinking, "What is the meaning of my life? Why am I here?

I've tried everything this world has to offer. Road kill. Chasing cats. Drinking toilet water. Still, there is an emptiness…."

No, dogs don't think things like that.

But people do.

All kinds of people, religious and non-religious, Christians and atheists, have pondered the meaning of our brief lives "under the sun," as Solomon put it. We wonder, "Why am I here? What will it take to fill the emptiness? Maybe if I just reached this goal, climbed that mountain, formed this relationship, or had this degree, life would take on new meaning."

In a sense, unless we've simply given up on life altogether, we're always moving forward, we're always on a quest. Why?

Because I think deep down we know that we were meant for another, better world. When we become Christians, we realize that our citizenship is in heaven and our life on earth just comes and goes, whether you live to be nine or ninety.

Solomon said, in essence, of our life on earth, "We are here only for a moment… Visitors and strangers in the land as our ancestors were before us. Our days on earth are like a shadow gone so soon without a trace" (I Chronicles 29:15, NLT).

The truth is, as Christians we are already citizens of heaven. So we long for something more. Paul wrote:

> But there's far more to life for us. We're citizens of high heaven! We're waiting the arrival of the Savior, the Master, Jesus Christ, who will transform our earthy bodies into glorious bodies like his own. He'll make us beautiful and whole with the same powerful skill by which he is putting everything as it should be, under and around him.
> (Philippians 3:20-21, THE MESSAGE)

It was Augustine who said of God, "You formed us for Yourself, and our hearts are restless until they find their rest in you."[70] Because of this, we want to know more about what is in our future and more about our heavenly home as we begin to see this world for what it is.

Just for a moment, let me distinguish what I mean when I say "the world," as opposed to speaking of "earth." We live on the earth. God

Himself created it, and both filled it and surrounded it with His handiwork. You can see His fingerprints everywhere. His signature is written across our planet and all of the wonderful things that He has made.

The Bible says, "The earth is the LORD's, and everything in it" (Psalms 24:1, NLT). Paul reminds us that we are not "to trust in uncertain riches but in the living God, who gives us richly all things to enjoy" (1 Timothy 6:17).

I believe that Christians, more than anyone else, have the capacity to appreciate a beautiful sunset, a rainbow, or a night sky filled with radiant stars, because we know the One who created it all, and we have an intimate relationship with Him.

That's "the earth."

But sometimes we speak about "the world."

When Christians refer to the world, they're often speaking of a godless world system that is under control of Satan, "the god of this world," and "the prince of the power of the air." And the closer we get to God, the better we begin to see the world for what it truly is and has become.

In his first letter to the church, the apostle John wrote:

> Don't love the world's ways. Don't love the world's goods. Love of the world squeezes out love for the Father. Practically everything that goes on in the world—wanting your own way, wanting everything for yourself, wanting to appear important— has nothing to do with the Father. It just isolates you from him. The world and all its wanting, wanting, wanting is on the way out—but whoever does what God wants is set for eternity. (1 John 2:15-17, THE MESSAGE)

Deep down inside, we long for a place we have never been to before. C. S. Lewis wrote:

> There have been times when I think we do not desire heaven, but more often I find myself wondering in our heart of hearts if we have ever desired anything else. It is the secret signature of each soul. The incommunicable and unappeasable want.[71]

I'm reminded of the story of a little boy who was flying his kite. Apparently, he had plenty of string, because as the kite went up higher and higher, he eventually lost sight of it altogether. About that time a man came along and saw the boy holding onto the string.

"What are you doing?" he said.

"I'm flying my kite," the boy replied.

The man looked up and said, "I can't see your kite anywhere. How do you know it's even there?"

"I *know* it's there," the boy replied, "because I can feel its tug."

In the same way, you and I know there is a heaven because we can feel its tug. It goes back to the earliest days of our childhood. And I will tell you this: When you know someone who is already there, heaven becomes much more important, and much more real.

But thoughts of heaven aren't only for people who have recently lost loved ones, or who are getting on in years and adjusting to a new reality. Actually, all of us should be thinking aggressively about heaven. And here's why. In the book of Colossians, Paul writes: "Since, then, you have been raised with Christ, set your hearts on things above, where Christ is seated at the right hand of God. Set your minds on things above, not on earthly things" (Colossians 3:1-2, NIV).

To "set your mind" speaks of a diligent, active, single-minded investigation—as if you had lost something and were searching for it.

That is how we should be looking at heaven.

Another way to translate this verse is simply, "Think heaven." The verb used in this verse is in the present tense, which could be translated, "Keep seeking heaven."

What is Paul saying? He's saying that we who belong to Jesus Christ should constantly keep seeking and thinking about heaven. Our feet must be on earth, but our minds must be in heaven.

Even so, many of us will go through a day—or even a week—without a single thought of heaven. E. M. Bounds made this statement:

> Heaven ought to draw and engage us. Heaven ought to so fill our thoughts, our hands, our conversations, our character, and our features that all would see that we are foreigners and strangers to this world. The very atmosphere of this world should be chilling to us and noxious. Its suns eclipsed and its companionship dull and

insipid. Heaven is our native land and it is home to us. Death to us is not the dying hour but the birth hour.[72]

What a great quote.

And it was Warren Wiersbe who said, "For the Christian, heaven isn't a simply a destination. It is a motivation."[73]

But *how* are you and I to be thinking about heaven, a place where we have never been? What's our point of reference? One of our problems is that we may have a caricatured version of heaven in our brain. Even though we may know better, we kind of imagine going to heaven, having wings sprout on our backs, and floating around through the clouds and the mist with a golden harp.

First of all, people don't become angels. Only angels are angels. And we will certainly not sit around on fluffy clouds spending eternity in endless boredom. That's about as far from the mark as you could possibly get. We need to understand what the Bible actually has to say about our future, eternal home.

What is Heaven Like?

Periodically, people will write books about their alleged experiences of dying, going to heaven, and returning to earth. I was looking at one just recently, and found it fascinating.

Are they true? Any of them?

Who knows? The only way I would say outright that some account of a heavenly visit wasn't true would be if it contradicted Scripture. But even if it didn't contradict Scripture, I would read it with interest and say, "Well, maybe that's true, and maybe it isn't. Maybe they're making it up, and maybe they're not."

What I need—what we all need—is a more authoritative source. And of course that takes me to the pages of the Scripture, so I can know how to think when I think about heaven.

What is Heaven?

Heaven is the dwelling place of God Himself.

In a broad sense, of course, God is everywhere. We use the word omnipresent, which basically means that wherever you go, God is already there.

The psalmist said it like this:

> I can never escape from your spirit!
> I can never get away from your presence!
> If I go up to heaven, you are there;
> if I go down to the place of the dead, you are there.
> If I ride the wings of the morning,
> if I dwell by the farthest oceans,
> even there your hand will guide me,
> and your strength will support me.
> (Psalm 139:7-10, NLT)

So yes, on one hand, God is everywhere. On the other hand, God has chosen to dwell in heaven in all of His glory. I believe that when we find ourselves longing for heaven, we're really longing for God Himself.

In the Psalms, David cried out, "O God, you are my God; I earnestly search for you. My soul thirsts for you; my whole body longs for you in this parched and weary land where there is no water" (Psalm 63:1, NLT).

Sounds like he's homesick to me. Homesick for heaven, and homesick for the God of heaven.

In his wonderful book *Heaven*, author Randy Alcorn makes this statement:

> We may imagine we want a thousand different things, but God is the only One we really long for. His presence brings satisfaction. His absence brings thirst and longing. Our longing for heaven is a longing for God. Being with God is the heart and soul of heaven. Every other heavenly pleasure will derive from and be secondary to His presence.

He concludes, "God's greatest gift to us is and always will be Himself."[74]

We long to be with God. We long to see God. And yet if God were to show Himself to us today we wouldn't be able to handle it. We would melt like a Popsicle on a hot sidewalk—or simply disintegrate on the spot. Why? Because God is perfect and flawless and holy… and I am imperfect and flawed and unholy.

One day Moses, the man of God, said to the Lord, "Show me your glory." God said, "No. I can't do that for you. But I will let you see Me as I pass by. You can sort of catch the afterglow." Why? Because God knew that no one could see Him and live.[75]

But there is a day coming when we *will* see God. Jesus said so. In His Sermon on the Mount He said, "Blessed are the pure in heart, for they shall see God" (Matthew 5:8). In a burst of faith, right in the midst of his grief and suffering, Job cried out, "But as for me, I know that my Redeemer lives, and that he will stand upon the earth at last. And after my body has decayed, yet in my body I will see God! I will see him for myself. Yes, I will see him with my own eyes. I am overwhelmed at the thought!" (Job 19:25-26, NLT). When will you see God? When you get to heaven. As Asaph says, "Whom have I in heaven but you? And earth has nothing I desire besides you" (Psalm 73:25, NIV).

Seeing God will be like seeing everything we have ever seen for the first time. Why? Because not only will we see God, but He will be the lens through which we will see everything else: people, ourselves, and all the varied events and ups and downs of this earthly life. When I see God, I will see everything. I will get it, and I will say, "Now, I understand."

What Do We Know About Heaven?

Heaven is an actual place.

It isn't an idea, a metaphor, an ideal, a philosophy, a happy thought, or a state of mind.

No, it's an *address*.

I can't relate to some spacey, weird, mystical dimension. I live in the real world. I am a real person. Tell me about real things. And heaven is a real place. More real than anything you and I have ever seen.

As He was preparing to depart this earth, Jesus told His grieving disciples, "I go to prepare a place for you" (John 14:2).

Most of us have heard the verse quoted from the King James Version that says, "In my Father's house are many mansions." The word mansion could be translated *dwelling place.* As to whether or not that is speaking of an actual residence that we will live in, or of the new body God will give us when we arrive, I don't know for sure.

But one thing is certain. Heaven is a place. A real place.

The late science fiction writer Isaac Asimov once wrote, "I don't believe in an afterlife, so I don't want to spend my whole life fearing hell or fearing heaven even more. For whatever the tortures of hell, I think the boredom of heaven would be even worse."[76]

What an unbelievably foolish statement.

For all his intelligence and success, Asimov had obviously done no research at all on the subject of heaven.

It will most certainly *not* be a boring place. It will be wonderful, exciting, and joyful beyond words. Remember Paul's words?

Eye has not seen, nor ear heard,
Nor have entered into the heart of man
The things which God has prepared for those who love Him.
(1 Corinthians 2:9)

Randy Alcorn writes:

Think of friends or family members who loved Jesus and are with Him now. Picture them with you walking together in this place. All of you have powerful bodies stronger than those of an Olympic athlete. You are laughing, playing, talking, reminiscing. You reach up to a tree to pick an apple or an orange. You take a bite. It is so sweet it is startling. You have never tasted anything so good. Now you see Someone coming towards you. It is Jesus with a big smile on His face. You fall to your knees in worship. He pulls you up and embraces you.[77]

Now, I understand that Randy is taking a little liberty there in painting that picture. But yet at the same time, everything that he said is based on Scripture. Heaven is a real place for real people who belong to God through faith in Jesus Christ, and the Bible uses a number of words to help describe it us.

Heaven is a Paradise

What do you think of when you think of Paradise?

As I cited earlier, the thief on the cross, dying beside Jesus, finally came to his senses and said, "Jesus, remember me when You come into your kingdom." And Jesus immediately responded, "I tell you the truth, today you will be with me in paradise" (Luke 23:42-43, NIV).

But what is this Paradise Jesus was speaking of?

Translated literally, that word in the first century would have been used to describe the garden of a king. It's almost impossible for us to imagine how luxurious and splendid a king's garden would appear to an average person in this era. If you were a relatively impoverished person and were unexpectedly given the privilege of stepping inside the walled and well-tended garden of a king, you would be overwhelmed by that experience. The fragrance and beauty of it all would blow your circuit breakers.

So "paradise" was a reference point for people—the best human language could do.

Imagine if you had the privilege of dying and going to heaven, and then at some point came back to earth to try and describe the experience. That's precisely what happened to the apostle Paul.

Try to imagine a group of people sitting around discussing the beautiful places they had visited. One guy says, "I've been to Hawaii, and I've never seen anything like it. The water is so blue, the sky is even bluer, and the air is balmy and warm. And oh—those soft trade winds that come in the evening. So wonderful."

The next guy says, "Yes, but have you ever been to Tahiti? Oh man, the water in Tahiti makes the water in Hawaii pale in comparison. It's an even deeper blue, and even warmer." Then a third guy says, "Well, I have been to the Seychelles Islands, and it's better than either Hawaii or Tahiti—the sky, the ocean, the flowers, the birds. It's the most beautiful place I've ever seen."

And then the apostle Paul could say, "Well, guys, I have been to heaven. And it is way better than all of those places you're talking about."

Paul actually went to heaven, and spoke about it—even if he didn't say as much about it as we might wish.

> I know a man who, fourteen years ago, was seized by Christ and swept in ecstasy to the heights of heaven. I really don't know if this took place in the body or out of it; only God knows. I also know that this man was hijacked into paradise—again, whether in or out of the body, I don't know; God knows. There he heard the unspeakable spoken, but was forbidden to tell what he heard.
> (2 Corinthians 12:2-3, THE MESSAGE)

I love that. Paul is saying, "I'm not really even sure what happened! I don't know if I was in the body or out of the body. All I can tell you is I can't even describe it."

But he does use one word.

Paradise.[78]

Heaven is a Place

Some would say, "We really can't know what heaven will be like, because it will simply be beyond our wildest dreams, so we have to leave it at that.

That is true, to a degree. But it's not totally true.

The apostle John, for instance, described heaven in great detail. Just listen to some of His words....

In Revelation 21 he says:

> The City shimmered like a precious gem, light-filled, pulsing light. She had a wall majestic and high with twelve gates. At each gate stood an Angel, and on the gates were inscribed the names of the Twelve Tribes of the sons of Israel: three gates on the east, three gates on the north, three gates on the south, three gates on the west. The wall was set on twelve foundations, the names of the Twelve Apostles of the Lamb inscribed on them. (vv. 11-14, THE MESSAGE)

It's obvious, isn't it? John is talking about a real place. Not just some weird, foggy land of nothingness. He goes on:

> The Angel speaking with me had a gold measuring stick to measure the City, its gates, and its wall. The City was laid out in a perfect square. He measured the City with the measuring stick: twelve thousand stadia, its length, width, and height all equal. Using the standard measure, the Angel measured the thickness of its wall: 144 cubits. The wall was jasper, the color of Glory, and the City was pure gold, translucent as glass. The foundations of the City walls were garnished with every precious gem imaginable: the first foundation jasper, the second sapphire, the third agate, the fourth emerald, the fifth onyx, the sixth carnelian, the seventh chrysolite, the eighth beryl, the ninth topaz, the tenth chrysoprase, the eleventh jacinth, the twelfth amethyst. The twelve gates were twelve pearls, each gate a single pearl.

> The main street of the City was pure gold, translucent as glass. But there was no sign of a Temple, for the Lord God—the Sovereign-Strong— and the Lamb are the Temple. The City doesn't need sun or moon for light. God's Glory is its light, the Lamb its lamp! The nations will walk in its light and earth's kings bring in their splendor. Its gates will never be shut by day, and there won't be any night. They'll bring the glory and honor of the nations into the City. Nothing dirty or defiled will get into the City, and no one who defiles or deceives. Only those whose names are written in the Lamb's Book of Life will get in. (Revelation 11:15-27, THE MESSAGE)

A real place. You'd better believe it.

In Revelation 22, John writes:

> Then the Angel showed me Water-of-Life River, crystal bright. It flowed from the Throne of God and the Lamb, right down the middle of the street. The Tree of Life was planted on each side of the River, producing twelve kinds of fruit, a ripe fruit each month. The leaves of the Tree are for healing the nations. (vv. 1-2, THE MESSAGE)

The reference to the Tree of Life goes all the way back to the Garden of Eden. After Adam and Eve ate of the tree the knowledge of good and evil, and sin entered the human race, they were forbidden to eat of the Tree of Life. Why? Because if they ate of it they would live forever in that fallen state. So the angels were sent to protect the Tree of Life from Adam and Eve, and Adam and Eve from the Tree of Life.

In heaven, however, that tree will be available to everyone.

Heaven is a City

Our eternal home is also described in Scripture as a city. In Hebrews 11:10 (NIV), the writer says that heaven is a "city with foundations, whose architect and builder is God." And then in Hebrews 13:14 (NIV) he adds: "For here we do not have an enduring city, but we are looking for the city that is to come."

Heaven…a city?

That's a bit hard for us to grasp, because we tend to think of cities as noisy, crowded places, with urban decay, graffiti, trash, and violent crime. But I want you to think of cities in a different way for a moment, if you would. Think of a perfect city where there is no crime, where everyone loves everyone, where the very streets and walls and sidewalks and buildings are translucent and glow with an inner radiance.

Cities have culture. Cities have art, music, goods, services, events, and restaurants. Restaurants in heaven? Why not? We know there will be feasting there.

Even earthly cities, for all their problems, have a certain unique quality to them. I think about Jerusalem at sunset, bathed in a golden light. Or Paris in springtime. Or morning in Rome.

These are all places and cities right here on our home planet. And heaven is a city, too. It is real, and we already have a placed reserved within its borders.

Heaven is a Country

Speaking of those who were persecuted or martyred for their faith, the author of Hebrews said: "But now they desire a better, that is, a heavenly country. Therefore God is not ashamed to be called their God, for He has prepared a city for them" (Hebrews 11:16).

A heavenly country. A land of indescribable beauty and infinite dimensions. Perhaps this is the ultimate fulfillment of the psalmist's desire: "He brought me out into a spacious place; he rescued me because he delighted in me" (Psalm 18:19, NIV).

You and I tend to think of earth as the "real thing," and heaven as the surreal thing. But it's the other way around. In reality, heaven is the real thing. When we're trying to get a handle on what heaven might be like, we tend to start with earth and reason up to heaven, when we ought to start with heaven and reason down toward earth.

Earth is the imitation, the "shadow lands," as C. S. Lewis called them. The temporary dwelling place. He said, "The hills and valleys of heaven will be to those we now experience not as a copy but as an original. Nor as the substitute is to the genuine article, but as the flower to the root or the diamond to the coal."[62]

There is an interesting statement in Hebrews 8:5 (NIV). The writer speaks of the priests of that day at the temple in Jerusalem, and notes that "They serve at a sanctuary that is a copy and shadow of what is in heaven."

A copy. A shadow. Could you say that about all of earth, as well as an earthly temple slated for imminent destruction?

The fact is, heaven will be infinitely better than anything we imagine, and Scripture only gives us tantalizing hints about what it will be like.

Minds on Heaven, Feet on Earth

So how should these thoughts about heaven affect us here on earth? Paul instructed us to "aim at and seek the [rich, eternal treasures] that are above, where Christ is, seated at the right hand of God" (Colossians 3:1, AMPLIFIED). In other words, our minds must be in heaven, but our feet must be on earth. How do we do that?

Let's go back to Colossians 3, where Paul continues:

Therefore put to death your members which are on the earth: fornication, uncleanness, passion, evil desire, and covetousness, which is idolatry. Because of these things the wrath of God is coming upon the sons of disobedience, in which you yourselves once walked when you lived in them.

But now you yourselves are to put off all these: anger, wrath, malice, blasphemy, filthy language out of your mouth. Do not lie to one another, since you have put off the old man with his deeds, and have put on the new man who is renewed in knowledge according to the image of Him who created him. (Colossians 3:5-10)

"Therefore…."

As I often say, whenever you see the word *therefore*, find out what it is there for. After telling us to seek heaven, think about heaven, and investigate heaven, Paul says, in effect, "Now…in light of all of this, here's how you ought to live."

It has been said of some people that they're "so heavenly minded they are no earthly good." I think there are some people who are so earthly minded they are no heavenly good. If you are heavenly minded, in the best sense of that expression, you will be of the *greatest* earthly good.

If you are heavenly minded, it will affect the way you live on earth. And if heaven doesn't affect the way you live your daily life, just how heavenly minded could you really be?

As he develops that thought, Paul deals with three categories of sins that you might say keep us "earthbound," grounded, and miserable.

Sins that Keep Us Earthbound

Sexual sin keeps us earthbound.

In Colossians 3, verse 5, Paul uses the word "fornication," which is from the Greek word *pornea*. We get our word "pornography" from that term, and it speaks of sexual immorality in general—including illicit sex, whether it is extramarital, homosexual, or premarital. In other words, all sex out of God's order.

And what is God's order? It's very, very important, but it isn't rocket science.

One man. One woman. Marriage.

That's it. That is His order. And it applies not only to our actions, but to our *thoughts* as well.

Jesus said, "You have heard the commandment that says, 'You must not commit adultery.' But I say, anyone who even looks at a woman with lust has already committed adultery with her in his heart" (Matthew 5:27-28, NLT). Oh, the Pharisees didn't like that. They prided themselves on the fact that they didn't commit the actual deed.

But Jesus said, in essence, "If you are thinking about it and fantasizing about it, it's the same thing."

It shouldn't surprise us, because the battle against sin—especially sexual sin—always begins in the mind. And if you don't win it there, you won't win it in the way that you live. Show me any person who has fallen into any kind of immorality, and I will show you a person who toyed with those things in his or her imagination—perhaps feeding those thoughts with pornography or trashy media or inappropriate conversations.

These are sins that will steal our joy and put the lights out on our testimony of life in Christ. And that's not how a citizen of heaven ought to live.

Idolatry keeps us earthbound.

In Colossians 3, verse 5, Paul calls covetousness idolatry. Isn't it interesting that the number one program in America (at this writing) is *American Idol*? I'm told that more people vote for their favorite idol candidate than vote for the president of the United States of America.

In the interest of full disclosure, it's a program I watch, too, on occasion…even though the title makes me uncomfortable.

What is an idol? *An idol is anyone or anything that takes the place of God in your life.* Everybody is a worshipper, whether they claim to believe in God or not. Everyone worships someone or something. An idol is simply something that we allow to divert us from worshiping, walking with, obeying, and serving the true and living God.

In other words, we can make a good thing into a bad thing by moving it from its proper and rightful place in our lives. A car can be an idol. A house can be an idol. Your career can be your idol. A college degree could be an idol. A boyfriend or a girlfriend could be an idol. Your child could be an idol. There any number of things we might put in the place of that belongs to God alone.

If you are dedicated to something, passionate about it, and can't stop thinking about it so that it becomes the primary interest or love in your life, that thing in effect becomes your god.

What, then, does Paul mean when he says that covetousness is idolatry? What does it mean to covet? Actually, "covet" is an interesting term. It comes from two root words which are "to have" and "more."

To have more. (And more and more and more.) It's the sin of never being satisfied or content, but always wanting more.

It starts with kids. Child A has a toy that Child B wants to play with. Child B bonks Child A on the head, and then claims the toy. After a few minutes, Child B abandons the toy and moves on. (It was more the thrill of the hunt, I think, than the actual toy.)

Then we grow up and we become adults. And one day you say, "You know what…I'm tired of my husband. I like *her* husband. I want him." So you go get him. And then you hear yourself saying, "You know what? My other husband was better than this guy. What am I doing here with this loser?" In the process, of course, lives and marriages and homes and families are destroyed—perhaps for generations.

Coveting is a serious life issue…and quickly becomes idolatry. This is not how a heavenly-minded person ought to live.

Anger, meanness, and slander keep us earthbound.

In Colossians 3, verse 8, the apostle goes on with other things that can keep us from living like citizens of heaven:

> But now you yourselves are to put off all these: anger, wrath, malice, blasphemy, filthy language out of your mouth.

Anger in this context speaks of a settled and habitual anger, mixed in with thoughts of revenge. This isn't a person who just gets a little ticked off and then gets over it. This is a person who says, "I don't get mad, I get even." You need to stop that. That is inappropriate behavior for a citizen of heaven.

Wrath speaks of a boiling agitation of the feelings. Sudden, violent anger. In context, the word *blasphemy* here is not speaking so much of blaspheming God as much as it is talking about slandering others.

We are a culture that is obsessed with gossip. The very word "gossip" makes a hissing sound, doesn't it? *Gossssssip*. Just like a serpent. We all fall into this trap from time to time; we can find it kind of enjoyable to be spreading negative information about someone else. But it isn't so much fun when you find out that someone has been gossiping or telling lies about you. Don't let this be part of your lifestyle as a child of God…and as a citizen of heaven.

Let me offer a fresh way to look at these all-too-human struggles. You don't need to *turn away* from something as much as you need to *turn to* another. What do you do when you want a child to let go of something? You put something better and more interesting in front of him—and he will let go in a hurry to reach for that new something.

You and I need something that is more important to us than the earthly attractions that keep tripping us up. As one old preacher put it, we need "the expulsive power of a new affection." I like that phrase. This new affection causes that old thing to be seen for what it is, and I don't want it any more.

What is the new affection?

Heaven.

I want to be a heavenly-minded person. That simply means I desire to be a person who thinks about God and wants what God wants more than anything else. Yes, I'm still a real person living a real life on the earth. But at the same time, I'm not letting the worries and cares and preoccupations of life on earth become the most important things in my life.

I have higher priorities.

I want that expulsive power of a new affection, where I am loving God, and therefore I don't want to be tied up with the love of this world.

If you have asked Christ to come into your life you are now His child, you are a citizen of heaven. It's time to start living like one, because this life is fading like a puff of vapor in the wind. Sooner than any of us imagine, we'll be stepping into eternity.

Don't waste your precious life God has given to you. Make every year, every month, every week, every day, indeed every hour, count for Him.

C. S. Lewis said it best: "Aim at heaven and you will get earth thrown in. Aim at earth and you will get neither."[79]

Makes sense, doesn't it?

Chapter Twelve

WHAT WILL WE DO IN HEAVEN?

But you have come to Mount Zion, to the heavenly Jerusalem, the city of the living God. You have come to thousands upon thousands of angels in joyful assembly, to the church of the firstborn, whose names are written in heaven.
—Hebrews 12:22-23, NIV

Even with my GPS device in my car, I seem to be navigationally challenged. Maybe my trouble is that I try to outguess it. The GPS will try to guide me to such-and-such a freeway, but I'm thinking to myself, *I know a better way than that.* But then it keeps telling me I've made a mistake and need to get off or go back… or maybe get a life.

I actually read about a motorist in the Midwest who followed his GPS directions onto a snowmobile trail, got stuck in the snow, and had to dial 911. The officer who responded said, "People shouldn't believe everything these gadgets tell you."

We think we're pretty smart as a culture, because we've invented this global positioning technology. But the truth is, what we've invented isn't half as amazing as the sophisticated homing instincts God has built into certain animals and birds.

I read about one species of bird known as the Manx Shearwater, that make their nests somewhere off the coast of Wales. Scientists took a number of these birds, tagged them, and released them at different points around the globe to see whether they could find their way back home to the Coast of Wales.

And they did. All of them. Within twelve days, they were back.

One bird in particular made it all the way from Boston, traveling 250 miles a day from a place it had never been before to get back home. Now that's what you call a homing instinct!

Another bird, the Golden Plover, is native to the Hawaiian Islands, but migrates every summer to the Aleutian Islands off of Alaska, some 1,200 miles away. I guess the Plover thinks Hawaii gets a little too hot in the summer—or maybe it's fed up with all the tourists, and says, "Let's go to the Aleutians for awhile."

When they arrive after their long trip, they mate, lay their eggs, and their little fledglings are born. And then the parent birds say, "See ya. Come visit." And they fly back to Hawaii, leaving the little fledglings to fend for themselves. Then, when a certain time of year rolls around, the young birds somehow know how to make a 1,200 mile journey to Hawaii, a place they have never been before.

Without question, these birds have a God-given GPS—a homing instinct from the Lord.

Guess what? God has placed a homing instinct in you and me as well. But it's not a homing instinct for the Hawaiian or Aleutian islands.

Ours is homing instinct for eternity.

Or another way to put it, it's a homesickness for heaven. We are pre-wired to long for a place we have never been before. Again, as we are told in the book of Ecclesiastes, "God has placed eternity in our hearts."[81]

Made for Another World

Heaven is the real deal, the eternal dwelling place of every follower of Jesus Christ. C. S. Lewis wrote,

All the things that have ever deeply possessed your soul have been hints of heaven—tantalizing glimpses, promises never quite fulfilled, echoes that died away just as they caught your ear. If I find in myself a desire which no experience in this world can satisfy, the most probably explanation is I was made for another world.

Lewis concludes, "Earthly pleasures were never meant to satisfy, but to arouse, to suggest, the real thing."[82]

Yes, heaven is the real thing that we long for.

But questions often arise, and we wonder about heaven. Let's consider a few of these questions.

What Will Our New Bodies be Like?

God is going to give you a brand new body, but it won't be unrelated to your existing body. The blueprint for your eternal, glorified body is in the body you now possess. It's already there. There will be a connection between the Greg Laurie of earth and the Greg of heaven. And the same is true for all of us.

Job said, "And after my skin has been destroyed, yet in my flesh I will see God; I myself will see him with my own eyes—I, and not another" (Job 19:26, NIV).

The Bible promises that these bodies of ours will be resurrected, and there will be that unmistakable connection and correlation between the old and the new. Heaven is the earthly life of the believer, glorified and perfected.

For all its similarities, however, there will be wonderful differences.

When we get to the other side, our minds and our memories will be clearer than they have ever been before. Paul tells us in 1 Corinthians 15 says, "Our bodies now disappoint us."

Amen to that! But here's the whole reference:

Our bodies now disappoint us, but when they are raised, they will be full of glory. They are weak now, but when they are raised, they will be full of power. They are natural human bodies now, but when they are raised, they will be spiritual bodies. (1 Corinthians 15:43-44, NLT)

That means that our new bodies will in some ways be the same as our old bodies, but at the same time they will be different. Without question they will be radically improved. No more physical disabilities. No signs of age. No sinful tendencies.

Joni Eareckson Tada, who has had to endure a paralyzed body for over forty years, says this about our new bodies:

No more bulging middles or balding tops. [Thank you, Joni!] No varicose veins or crow's feet. No more cellulite or support hose. Forget the thunder thighs and the highway hips. Just a quick leapfrog over the tombstone and it is a body you have always dreamed of. Fit and trim. Smooth and sleek.[83]

In fact, our new, resurrection bodies will resemble the resurrection body of Jesus Christ. As we know, Christ was crucified and rose again from the dead three days later. And we know that after His resurrection He walked around in a real physical body. You could touch Him. He ate fish in front of everyone, the Bible says. And yet He could appear in a room without using the door. And of course, He ascended to glory.

Will we be able to do the same things? I don't know. But the Bible does say in 1 John 3:2, "Beloved, now we are the children of God; and it has not yet been revealed what we shall be, but we know that when He is revealed, we will be like Him, for we will see Him as He is."

Do you long for that day? Do you look forward to that moment when you will see the Lord face to face?

Life goes by so quickly. Billy Graham was asked awhile back what the greatest surprise of his life had been. He answered: "The brevity of it."[84]

When you're young, it seems like life goes on forever. When I was in elementary school, it seemed like each school day lasted months. I still have one of my old report cards for those days. The teacher wrote on it: "Greg spends too much time looking out the window and daydreaming and drawing cartoons. He will never amount to anything."

At least part of that was true: I did a lot of daydreaming and looking out the window...watching the clock and wondering why it wasn't working.

But then when you get out of elementary school, junior high goes a little bit faster. Then high school (it flies by). And then adult life. And then pretty soon you start remembering decades instead of years. Then one day you look in the mirror and you hardly recognize the old person looking back at you! *When did that happen? When did I get old?*

I started getting AARP magazines delivered to my house recently. I didn't ask for that, and I really don't want it. But then someone told me that because of my age, which is 57, that I now qualify for a discount at the movie theater as a senior citizen. And guess what? I am taking advantage of it. Why not?

But there are those telltale signs that you are getting old. You know you are getting old when you get winded playing chess. You know you are getting old when you try to straighten the wrinkles in your socks, and then you realize you're not wearing any. You know you are getting old when your pacemaker accidently opens the garage door. You know you are getting old when you bend over to tie your shoes, and then wonder what else you can do while you're down there. You know you are getting old when you actually look forward to a dull evening at home. You know you are getting old when your mind makes commitments that your body can't keep. You know you are getting old when someone calls you at 9:00 in the evening, and says, "Did I wake you?" You know you are getting old when your ears are hairier than your head!

So often we think of ourselves as a body that happens to have a soul. But the reality is, you are a soul wrapped in a body. Yes, your body is "the real you." But there is more than your body! The thing that gives you spark and personality is your soul, the part of you that lives forever in the presence of God.

Will We Recognize One Another in Heaven?

The short answer is yes. Absolutely.

Why would you think that you would know less in heaven than you know on earth? In heaven, we will be perfected. Glorified. In fact, in 1 Corinthians 13:12 it says, "I shall know as I am known." There will be no more mysteries. No more questions. Everything will be resolved. You will *know*. Will you still love your family and friends? Of course you will! In fact, it will be a stronger, purer, and sweeter love.

Death breaks ties on earth but it renews them in heaven. And we will be the same people in heaven that we were on earth. We don't become a different person. You are still you and I am still me, but the *perfected* version of me, without all the flaws, shortcomings, and sinful tendencies.

Do you remember the story in John 17, where Jesus appeared on the Mount of Transfiguration with Moses and Elijah? Did you ever wonder how it was that everyone knew it was Moses and Elijah, without their saying so? Do you think Moses was standing there with the stone tablets under his arm, or that maybe Elijah was calling down fire from heaven? Or do you imagine they had one of those newcomer badges people wear, that said, "Hi, I'm Moses"?

No. I don't think so. Somehow, they were simply recognizable, and the men on the mountain with Jesus that day knew instantly who they were. I believe it will be the same for us in heaven. Somehow, I don't think there will need to be lengthy introductions, "icebreakers," get-acquainted sessions, when we first arrive.

I love the way Jesus stated it after He rose from the dead and met with His followers. He said, "It is I myself! Touch me and see" (Luke 24:39, NIV).

It's Me, guys. It wasn't a different Jesus. It was (and is) the same Jesus in a glorified body.

But What Will We Do in Heaven?

Why do we even ask this question? Because we think about the word "forever" and we fear that we'll soon be bored. Someone will say, "Am I just going to sit around on a cloud, strum a harp now and then, and sleep?"

That might sound nice to some, but not to me! So it's good news to know there will actually be activities in heaven. One of the things you will be doing in heaven is worshipping God. And by the way, that is why you were created in the first place—to bring honor and glory to your Creator. In a sense, we will be reclaiming our original purpose, one that was so distorted and damaged by the fall.

I feel pretty certain that in our perfected, eternal bodies, we will all have perfect voices. No one will be going sharp or flat. We will harmonize perfectly as we sing the praises of God. Here's what we read in Revelation 15:

> I saw before me what seemed to be a crystal sea mixed with fire. And on it stood all the people who had been victorious over the beast and his statue and the number representing his name. They were all holding harps that God had given them. And they were singing the song of Moses, the servant of God, and the song of the Lamb:

> "Great and marvelous are your actions,
> Lord God Almighty.
> Just and true are your ways,
> O King of the nations.
> Who will not fear, O Lord, and glorify your name?
> For you alone are holy.
> All nations will come and worship before you,
> for your righteous deeds have been revealed."
> (vv. 2-4, NLT)

Maybe one of the reasons we will be able to sing out without hesitation in heaven will be because our problems, sorrows, conflicts, and worries will be gone. All of our questions will be answered and resolved.

One of the reasons we have a hard time worshipping on earth is because we don't always "feel like it."

We will say, "I'm not in the mood to worship right now. I think I have a cold." Or, "I have this situation in my life that's weighing on me right now, so I don't really feel like singing praises to God." Or we may even allow ourselves to be critics of the worship service, even while it's underway. "I didn't really like that worship set as much as last week's—it was a little too loud." Or, "I've never liked that instrument. I don't know why they keep using it."

Yes, we all have our preferences and prejudices. But worship isn't something we should critique, it is something we should *do*, and we should do it whether we feel like it or not, or whether we are in the ideal circumstances or not.

That is why the Bible talks about the "sacrifice of praise" (Hebrews 13:15) because there are times when praise is a sacrifice. I don't *want* to offer it, my flesh resists offering it, but I offer it anyway because I know that God is in control. I know that He loves me, and that He is worthy of my praise. So I offer it up.

Let me be straightforward here. *Worship is not about you, it's about Him.* If we can keep that in mind when we sing our praises to God, it can make all the difference in the world.

Yes, we will worship the Lord when we are in heaven, but we won't worship all the time. Sometimes people have this idea that we'll just be laying on our stomachs worshipping for eons. Yes, we will certainly worship. But we will also be busy, traveling across the new heavens and the new earth (at the speed of thought) doing our Father's business.

The Bible tells us in Revelation 7:15 that the Lord's saints "are standing in front of the throne of God, serving him day and night in his Temple. And he who sits on the throne will live among them and shelter them" (NLT).

Serving Him…how?

Who knows? But we you can bet that it will be the most exciting, fulfilling, joyous experience you have ever known.

Yes, heaven is a place of rest, but I can only rest for so long. It will also be a place of productivity. One wonders what the Lord has in store for us when we get there. We wonder if we will be able to perhaps finish some of the tasks that remain uncompleted on earth. Maybe you had dreams that were shattered here, that will in some sense be fulfilled there. Sometimes we act as though anything and everything that can be done must be done while we're still on earth.

Now of course, we do want to make the most of time on earth. We don't determine when we are born, nor do we determine when we die. But we have everything to do with that little dash in the middle, the thin line on our memorial stone that marks the years between our birth and our passing. But I would simply remind us that life does not end after life on earth. It continues on in heaven.

And the best is yet to come.

Some of our earthly lives will be limited by disability or illness. Some of our lives will be cut short through death. Some of us will have our expected productivity short-circuited because of physical or emotional or circumstantial reasons, and we won't realize our fondest dreams on this side of heaven. Who is to say that God would not allow us to complete what He inspired us to start on the other side?

Remember that verse in Philippians? "He who began a good work in you will carry it on to completion until the day of Christ Jesus" (Philippians 1:6, NIV). God is all about finishing what He begins.

Granted, it is frustrating because we meet some people who live long lives that are squandered and wasted. And then we see someone with so much promise and ability and gifting die unexpectedly, and we think that is so unfair. That's because we are putting all of our thinking into life on earth, and not realizing that life goes on.

Death for the believer is *not* the end of life but a continuation of it in another place. You *will* live forever. Don't forget that. Earth is like a stopover.

When I'm flying, I don't like stopovers at all.

Whenever I book a flight I try to get a direct flight, because sometimes during stopovers, bad things happen. Inclement weather rolls in and you get stuck, or the scheduled flight crew doesn't show up, or whatever. So I like to get from A to B as quickly as possible.

Nevertheless, life on earth is a stopover. An airport lounge. A bus terminal. A train station. We're not at our destination yet, but we're on our way. And the last stage of that journey won't be long at all. It will come much sooner than we may realize.

What else will we do in heaven?

We're going to eat!

Revelation 19:9 (NIV) says, "Blessed are they that are invited to the Wedding Supper of the Lamb."

I like the fact that the word supper is used. Here in California, where I live, we usually refer to the evening meal as "dinner." In the South, however, it's "supper." They will say, "Wash up for supper!"

I heard this a lot growing up, because for a good part of my childhood I was raised by my grandparents Stella and Charles, who were from Arkansas.

I called my grandmother Mama Stella and my grandfather Daddy Charles. My grandmother, I'm happy to say, was from the old school of home cooking. Mama Stella never saw a TV dinner, never reheated anything, and didn't care much for processed foods period. She made everything from scratch. I can still close my eyes and taste that fresh fried chicken. And of course, all of those fresh vegetables—string beans, black-eyed peas, okra, collard greens, and real mashed potatoes.

Grandma Stella's crowning achievement was her biscuits. I have never had one as good since she went to heaven. And it strikes me as perfectly logical that the Lord would employ her abilities in heaven at the supper of the Lamb.

But we will also be able to sit down with the great saints of old. Matthew 8:11 (NIV) says, "I tell you this, that many Gentiles will come from all over the world and sit down with Abraham, Isaac, and Jacob at the feast in the Kingdom of Heaven."

Can you even imagine this? Sitting at a table and saying, "Moses, excuse me, would you please pass the manna?" Or maybe, "Elijah, my meat is a little undercooked. Would you get a little extra fire on it?"

Imagine being able to pick the brain of some great man or woman of faith, and find out all about him or her. Talk to Mary about having the Son of God conceived in her womb. Talk to Moses about seeing the Red Sea parted. Talk to Noah about the ark. Talk to Shadrach, Meshach, and Abednego about the fiery furnace. ("Did you guys use sunscreen?") Talk to Daniel about the lion's den. The list goes on, and how amazing it will be.

The thing biggest in my heart right now, however, will be the opportunity to reunite with loved ones. I think especially of my son Christopher, who as I mentioned earlier went to be with the Lord in

2008 at the age of thirty-three. Needless to say, I miss him very much, and look forward to seeing him with all my heart.

When Christopher was just a boy and I would carry him around, he was always a curious little guy, and he would point to things and ask me what they were. And because he was very little he didn't say, "What's that?" He just said "S'at."

He would point to a truck. "S'at—?"

"That's a truck."

"S'at—?"

"That's a tree."

"S'at—?"

"That's another tree."

"S'at—?"

"That's a house."

He said it over and over, *S'at. S'at. S'at*, until it really began to wear me out.

So now, Topher (his nickname) has gone on to heaven ahead of me. And after I arrive and we're walking around together, I will say, "S'at—?"

"That's the sea of glass, Dad."

"S'at—?"

"That's an angel, Dad."

"When do eat dinner?"

"Any time, Dad."

But the main event of heaven will be Jesus. Yes, we long for heaven, but what we are really longing for is God Himself. Jesus said, "When everything is ready, I will come and get you, so that you will always be with me where I am" (John 14:3, NLT).

Paul said, "Sometimes I long to go and be with Christ. That would be far better for me" (Philippians 1:23, NLT).

D. L. Moody wrote, "It is not the jeweled walls and pearly gates that are going to make heaven attractive. It is being with God."[85]

God will be there. You can ask Him anything, tell Him anything, and hear everything He has to say to you. You will have all the time in the world when you get to heaven. It is our future home, the place we desire and long for with a homing instinct we can't explain any other way.

When I travel, I start missing home almost as soon as I leave the ground. If you are overseas very long, you long for your country, you long for your house, you long for your bed, and you certainly long for your family.

And in the same way, we all long for our home in heaven.

Years ago Audio Adrenaline recorded a song called "Big House," about heaven. They sang it at one of our crusades years ago. Speaking of heaven they sang:

> It's a big, big house
> with lots and lots of room,
> A big, big table
> with lots and lots of food,
> A big, big yard
> where we can play football,
> A big, big house
> It's my Father's house

Steven Curtis Chapman, a contemporary Christian recording artist lost his little adopted daughter Maria in an accident in 2008, the same year we lost Christopher.

Maria was adopted from China, and he was able to speed up the adoption process because Maria had been born with a hole in her heart. And Steven and his wife Mary Beth loved her with all their hearts. She was a beloved part of the family.

In a recent radio broadcast, Steven spoke with Dr. Dobson about that event. Within the interview, he mentioned a postcard I had written to him that I never knew he had received. It surprised me when I heard him mention it. And in my card I had told him that his little girl was going to be much more a part of his future than his past. He told Dr. Dobson that the thought encouraged him very much.

He also related a story about when little Maria came to his wife Mary Beth, and asked her about this place she had heard about in

Sunday School. She had heard about a "big, big house, with lots and lots of food, and a big, big yard, and so forth." Immediately, Mary Beth recognized that little Maria was talking about that Audio Adrenaline song. So she said, "Oh, you mean where we will play football?"

"Yeah, Mommy. That is the place."

"Well, that is a song about heaven."

Little Maria said, "I want to go to there."

And of course Mommy said, "Well, one day. Later. Not any time soon."

But the Lord had prepared this little girl, and that is where she is now. In heaven. In that big, big house, sitting at that big, big table. I don't know about the football part. But then again...why not?

A Prepared Place for Prepared People

If I plan on taking a plane trip, I have to first book a ticket. I don't just walk into the airport and walk onto a plane. In the same way, if you want to be sure you're going to heaven, you need the ticket.

You say, "How much will it cost?"

You couldn't afford it. Not in a million years.

But the good news is that Jesus Christ came to this earth and died on a cross for your sin and rose again from the dead, and in effect purchased your ticket for heaven and eternal life. Here is how you receive it. You just say, "Lord, I accept that gift that You have offered to me. I turn from my sin and I put my faith in You."

If you have done that, then you have a reserved place and a future home that no one can ever take away from you. As Peter said, "Now we live with great expectation, and we have a priceless inheritance— an inheritance that is kept in heaven for you, pure and undefiled, beyond the reach of change and decay" (1 Peter 1:3-4, NLT).

It's a big, big house.

And more than anywhere else in the universe, it is where you belong.

Chapter Thirteen

DOWN TO EARTH TALK ABOUT HEAVEN

"Do not let your heart be troubled; believe in God, believe also in Me. In My Father's house are many dwelling places; if it were not so, I would have told you; for I go to prepare a place for you." —John 14:1-2, NASB

Sometimes it's difficult for us to wrap our minds around this eternal destination called heaven.

What will it be like for us? Will it seem strange? Will it really feel like home? The mental pictures we conjure up seem so surreal, so mystical, so misty and foggy at times.

But there is nothing misty or foggy about heaven. The Bible presents heaven as a future destination, identifying it as a real place, and a home that will be inexpressibly better than anything we are experiencing now. The Bible promises that in heaven we will be given new bodies that will be strong and healthy, and that we will never have to deal with pain or sorrow or fear again.

As I talk to people about our life in the presence of God, however, three or four questions invariably surface. You might call them down-to-earth questions about a beyond-the-earth reality.

Let's consider them one by one.

Question #1 Will We Still be Married in Heaven?

Some people would be very happy to think that there would be marriage in heaven. Others would not be so happy. So what's the answer?

It's really yes and no.

You will still have many of the relationships in heaven that you had on earth. Yes, you will be receiving a new body, made to last forever, and you will be relocating to heaven and ultimately to the new earth that God will establish. But that won't erase history. No, it will culminate history.

But what about the marriage relationship? Actually Jesus was asked that very question by a group of religious leaders known as the Sadducees. Now this group of leaders, in contrast to the Pharisees, didn't believe in the resurrection of the dead or life after death.

Maybe that's where they got their name, because they were so sad… you see. It's a pretty bleak outlook to have no hope of life beyond the grave. This group of Jewish leaders thought they would trap Jesus with a hypothetical situation they'd dreamed up. Here's how it went:

> But that same day some of the Sadducees, who say there is no resurrection after death, came to him and asked, "Sir, Moses said that if a man died without children, his brother should marry the widow and their children would get all the dead man's property. Well, we had among us a family of seven brothers. The first of these men married and then died, without children, so his widow became the second brother's wife. This brother also died without children, and the wife was passed to the next brother, and so on until she had been the wife of each of them. And then she also died. So whose wife will she be in the resurrection? For she was the wife of all seven of them!" (Matthew 22:23-28, TLB)

With that question, these guys smugly supposed they had the Lord trapped, and that He wouldn't be able to answer. Jesus quickly put that idea to rest however, with His response.

> But Jesus said, "Your error is caused by your ignorance of the Scriptures and of God's power! For in the resurrection there is no marriage; everyone is as the angels in heaven." (Matthew 22: 29-30, TLB)

So…isn't that saying that we won't be married in heaven? Not necessarily. You won't be married to your spouse in heaven, but you will be married to the Lord, because the Bible clearly describes us as the bride of Christ. When we go to heaven, then, we will join our Groom, and in that sense there will be marriage on the other side.

But what about our relationship with our spouse? If you have been married to someone for 25, 35, 45, or 55 years, the idea of not having any connection with that husband or wife in eternity is troubling at the very least. But here's what you need to know. Your relationship with your spouse will not end. In heaven, Cathe and I will know each other. We won't be husband and wife in the same sense that we were on earth, but we will certainly still be in relationship.

Author Randy Alcorn puts it like this: "Earthly marriage is a shadow, an echo of the true and ultimate marriage. The purpose of marriage is not to replace heaven but to prepare us for it."[86]

The human institution of marriage culminates in heaven, and we will no longer be married in a technical sense. But that doesn't mean our relationship will end. God's plan for our lives doesn't stop in heaven, it continues. God doesn't abandon His purposes in heaven, He fulfills them. Therefore, friendships and relationships that have begun on earth will continue in heaven richer than ever.

Question #2 Do People in Heaven Know about Events on Earth?

Some people think those who have gone on before us know nothing of what is happening on earth. Others think they are watching everything. Sometimes people will even say, "I sense the presence of my loved one with me. I think he or she was guiding me during that difficult time."

Let me be a little blunt here, because we can't allow our emotions alone to guide us to unsound conclusions. The fact is, when a loved one dies and crosses over to heaven, you can no longer communicate with them, and they can no longer communicate with you. That doesn't mean there is no connection. It simply means there can be no real communication. People who are desperate to make contact with departed loved ones will reach out to psychics or mediums, wanting so much to have one last conversation or obtain one last word of advice.

The Bible says to have nothing to do with such things.

Here is what we need to know.

First, people in heaven may indeed be very aware of what is happening on earth.

In the Luke 16 passage we considered in an earlier chapter, we encountered the story of Lazarus and the rich man. Both men died, one going to a place of comfort in "Abraham's bosom," and the other to a place of torment on the other side. The rich man, suffering in Hades, was both fully conscious and aware of those he had left behind. In Luke 16:28, he expresses concern for his five brothers, not wanting them to end up where he was. If someone in hell was aware of relatives on earth, couldn't we conclude that it would be even more likely for someone in heaven?

Second, when people believe in Jesus on earth it is public knowledge in heaven.

In Luke 15, He gives us three vignettes about three things that are lost-and-found: a lost sheep, a lost coin, and finally, a lost son. The woman who found her lost coin and the shepherd who found his lost sheep rejoiced greatly over what had been restored to them. And Jesus adds these words: "I say to you that likewise there will be more joy in heaven over one sinner who repents than over ninety-nine just persons who need no repentance." And again, "Likewise, I say to you, there is joy in the presence of the angels of God over one sinner who repents" (Luke 15:7, 10).

Then finally it culminates with the parable of the prodigal son. You remember the story: the youngest son takes his share of the inheritance, leaves home, and blows it in riotous living. Then, reaching the bottom, he resolves to return home, and his father welcomes him with open arms.

I want you to notice something in this passage. Jesus doesn't say there will be joy *among* the angels over a sinner who repents, it says joy *in the presence of the angels.*

Could that be referring to those who have gone on before us as well as the angels? In heaven, we will know *more* than we know on earth, not less. Isn't it possible we could be aware of the fact that someone has placed faith in Christ because of our testimony? If there was a party breaking out in heaven, don't you think you would know about it?

I remember years ago we were in San Jose for one of our crusades, and I was staying in a hotel. I'm usually a light sleeper, so if there is noise in a room nearby, it's hard for me to fall asleep. We'd had an event that night, and the next night we were having another one, so I really wanted to get my rest.

In the room next to me, however, I heard music…that became louder and louder and louder. Pretty soon (and I'm not exaggerating) the bass speakers next door were moving the wall. *Thump. Thump. Thump.*

I thought, "This is crazy." So I finally called hotel security, and they called the police. It turns out there was a bachelor party going on in the room next door, with at least a hundred people in the room. It was complete with a DJ, sound system, and strobe lights. I watched through the little peephole in my door as the people began carting their equipment out of the room. They basically threw them out of the hotel.

Did I know there was a party going on? Was I aware of it?

You'd better believe it!

Now don't you think that if there was a celebration in heaven with angels singing and dancing or doing whatever they do to celebrate that you would be aware of it? Of course you would. Maybe you would even understand how your simple testimony had a part in that person's finally coming to Jesus Christ.

Third, people in heaven may know about the time and place of certain events on earth.

In Revelation 6 we read:

> When He opened the fifth seal, I saw under the altar the souls of those who had been slain for the word of God and for the testimony which they held. And they cried with a loud voice, saying, "How long, O Lord, holy and true, until You judge and avenge our blood on those who dwell on the earth?" Then a white robe was given to each of them; and it was said to them that they should rest a little while longer, until both the number of their fellow servants and their brethren, who would be killed as they were, was completed. (vv. 9-11)

I find it interesting how much these men and women seem to be aware of. These people are aware they were put to death on earth for their faith. They also seem to be conscious of the passing of time on earth. Why else would they say, "How long O Lord, holy and true, until You judge and avenge our blood…?" And they are given the answer that "they should rest a little while longer."

Notice also that there is some connection between the believers in heaven and those on earth. In Revelation 6:11, those in heaven are conversing about "their fellow servants and brothers" still on earth.

Fourth, those who have gone on before us may be cheering us on in our walk with Christ.
Listen to the writer of Hebrews:

> Since we have such a huge crowd of men of faith watching us from the grandstands, let us strip off anything that slows us down or holds us back, and especially those sins that wrap themselves so tightly around our feet and trip us up; and let us run with patience the particular race that God has set before us. (Hebrews 12:1-2, TLB)

The King James version speaks of our being "compassed about with so great a cloud of witnesses." Who are these witnesses? Are they the loved ones who have gone on before us, cheering us on from the grandstands of heaven?

Hebrews 12, of course, follows Hebrews 11, which many have described as "the hall of faith." It's something of a "who's who" of God's people, including names like Abraham, Moses, Joseph, Gideon, Samson, David, Rahab, and Daniel. In the first verse of Hebrews 12, the writer speaks of our being surrounded by a great cloud of witnesses. He seems to be saying, "In light of the fact that these men and women of God served the Lord so faithfully, you'd better run a good race, too."

The writer could be saying, "They have set a good pace. Follow it!" But he might also be saying, "These believers who have gone on before you are watching your progress." I don't think we can say for sure if they are or if they aren't. But we know for sure that our Lord Himself is watching our progress!

One Foot in Heaven?

There are things that can happen to us in this life that make us more aware of heaven and our future destination.

I was speaking with a lady the other day who has a severely

handicapped son, and caring for this boy has been extremely difficult for her. Referring to her son, she told me, "His life has placed one of my feet in heaven, and one on earth."

I understood what she was saying, and felt compassion for her. But when you think about it, that's not such a bad place to be.

The presence of pain and suffering can bring this about, as can the unexpected death of a loved one. You long to see that person, and you feel connected to heaven by stronger ties than you had ever experienced before.

C. S. Lewis once said, "A continual looking forward to the eternal world is not a form of escapism or wishful thinking, but one of the things a Christian is meant to do."[87]

For the believer, death is not only the great separator; in Jesus Christ, death is the great uniter. When we get to heaven we will not only be reunited with those that have gone before us, but we will be united with those we may have helped bring us to faith.

In 1 Thessalonians 2:19-20, the apostle writes: "For what is our hope, our joy, or the crown in which we will glory in the presence of our Lord Jesus when he comes? Is it not you? Indeed, you are our glory and joy" (NIV).

I love that! Paul is saying that these spiritual children of his will be his crown of rejoicing in the Lord's presence when He comes. This passage seems to be implying that when we get to heaven, we will in some sense have grouped around us those we helped to believe in Jesus.

Maybe that thought discourages you a little, instead of encouraging you. Maybe you would say, "I don't know that I have really helped that many people believe in Jesus."

The fact is, you really don't know how many people you have helped along in their journey of faith. You haven't seen the big plan, and you don't know how touching one person's life ended up touching another person's life and…on and on it goes. On this side of heaven, you and I don't really know how it will all play out.

The important thing is to simply be faithful with the opportunities that God sets before you. The truth is, you may have reached more people than you realize. Because ultimately it is God that converts people, not you or me. The Bible says that one sows, another waters, but it is God who gives the increase.[88] God is the one who brings men and women into the kingdom of God.

When you pray for the work of evangelism, you become invested in it. When you give financially to support the work of evangelism, you become invested in it. When you are kind to someone and help or bless someone in the name of Jesus, you become invested in evangelizing that life.

In fact, Jesus said, "I tell you the truth, anyone who gives you a cup of water in my name because you belong to Christ will certainly not lose his reward" (Mark 9:41, NIV).

The Judgment Seat of Christ

In an earlier chapter, we spoke about the terror of the final judgment known as the Great White Throne. That will be the dreadful moment when those who have rejected Jesus Christ and His forgiveness and salvation will have to stand before God and give an accounting of their lives.

How terrible will that be?

John wrote: "And I saw a great white throne and the one who sat upon it, from whose face the earth and sky fled away, but they found no place to hide" (Revelation 20:11 TLB).

We who believe in Jesus Christ, however, won't appear before that Great White Throne. We will already be in heaven, secure for all eternity. But the Bible does teach that each one of us will stand before the judgment seat of Christ, where He will dispense His rewards.

Maybe it would help to think of it more as an awards ceremony—like the Grammys or the Oscars.

Sometimes when you're watching the Academy Awards you find yourself pulling for a certain movie or a particular actor that you liked. And when that movie gets completely bypassed, you feel some disappointment.

In the same way, we may feel disappointed at times that our efforts or sacrifice or the investment of our time and skill goes unnoticed and unacknowledged. Granted, we do what we do for the Lord, and for His approval, not the approval of people. But even so, we're human, and it hurts sometimes to have our work or our best efforts get totally ignored.

At the judgment seat of Christ, our Lord takes care of that. Because God doesn't miss anything—not a single detail—of what we do for Him, or for others on His behalf. Jesus said, "Your Father who sees what is done in secret will reward you" (Matthew 6:6, NASB).

In 2 Corinthians 5:10, Paul says: "For we must all appear before the judgment seat of Christ, that each one may receive the things done in the body, according to what he has done, whether good or bad."

Somehow, this judgment will take place individual by individual. We will all have our appointment before the Lord, where He will review our lives. Don't imagine that God will at this time drag up all your old sins. He won't, because those sins are gone and forgotten! They have all been washed away and forgiven by the blood of Christ. And we should not choose to remember what God has chosen to forget.

That's not what this occasion will be about. It will be a time when the Lord will say to us, "What did you do with your life? What did you do with your resources? What did you do with your time and your opportunities?"

We all have one life, and the Lord will ask us how we invested what He gave us. It's possible for a believer to simply waste his or her opportunities on earth, instead of taking advantage of them. You can have a saved soul and a lost life.

The Bible tells us the story of the wicked King Belshazzar who was confronted by the prophet Daniel. Daniel looked the king in the eye and said, "You have been weighed in (God's) balances, and you have been found lacking" (Daniel 5:27).

Now normally, when we get on a scale we want to weigh less. But when you get on God's scales, you want to weigh more. You want to have substance and depth and purpose and weight to your life. Effectively Daniel was saying, "Belshazzar, you are a spiritual lightweight. You have done nothing with your life and all your wonderful privileges and opportunities."

Speaking of this judgment seat of Christ, Paul wrote:

> For no one can lay any other foundation than the one we already have—Jesus Christ. Now anyone who builds on that foundation may use gold, silver, jewels, wood, hay, or straw. But there is going to come a time of testing at the judgment day to see what kind of work each builder has done. Everyone's work will be put through the fire to see whether or not it keeps its value. If the work survives the fire, that builder will receive a reward. But if the work is burned up, the builder will suffer great loss. The builders themselves will be saved, but like someone escaping through a wall of flames.
> (1 Corinthians 3:11-15, NLT)

So the topic before Christ's throne at that time won't be so much about the bad things you've done, it's more about *what did you do with your life*? Did you accomplish anything? Did you impact anyone? Did you seek to glorify Me with your time and opportunities? Or did you spend it in empty pursuits and worthless activities?

I think most of us envision this day as being monopolized by the great heroes of the faith. As we ponder this awards ceremony, we think about people like Corrie ten Boom or Jim Elliot or Billy Graham. We imagine that these great men and women of God will get all the rewards, and there won't be anything left for us.

But I suggest to you there might be some surprises in heaven. I think we will also see the Lord reward some people you have probably never heard of before.

People like Pearle Goode.

Who is Pearle Goode? She was an older woman who heard of the ministry of Billy Graham, and committed herself to pray fervently for every crusade that he did. Word reached Billy Graham of the faithful prayers of this woman, and he was so moved by her ministry that they started flying her out to the crusades, so that she could pray on site. And that is what she faithfully did, until she passed away at the age of ninety. At her funeral service, Billy's wife Ruth paid this tribute to Pearl. She said, "Here lie the mortal remains of much of the secret of Bill's ministry."[89]

Pearle wasn't a preacher, missionary, or author. But while Billy did his part, Pearle did hers. While Billy was out preaching, Pearle was praying.

In the same way, you have your own part. So don't worry about what God has called someone else to do. Just focus on what God has called you to do, because the key in that final day is not how much you did but why you did it. God is far more interested in significance than He is in success. God is far more interested in faithfulness than He is in success.

In that final day, He won't say, "Well done, good and successful servant." No, He will say, "Well done, good and *faithful* servant...." It's all about faithfulness. It's all about doing what God has set before you, doing it well, and with all of your might. That is what we will be judged for in that final day.

At that time, crowns will be given out as rewards for faithful service.

As the grandfather of two little granddaughters, I am learning how little girls like to dress up like princesses. Having raised two boys, this is all new territory for me. Little girls love being Cinderella or Sleeping Beauty, with the full gown, the crown, the scepter, and the whole nine yards.

The crowns the Lord gives out on that day, however, won't be plastic or paper or aluminum. They will be eternal, and beautiful beyond description.

There will be a crown of rejoicing.

Paul wrote to the Thessalonians, "For what is our hope, or joy, or crown of rejoicing? Is it not even you in the presence of our Lord Jesus Christ at His coming? For you are our glory and joy" (1 Thessalonians 2:19-20).

This will probably be a soul-winners crown, for those who have used their influence for the glory of God.

There will be a crown of life.

James writes: "Blessed is the man who perseveres under trial, because when he has stood the test, he will receive the crown of life that God has promised to those who love him" (James 1:12, NIV).

This crown is specifically promised for the man or woman who has resisted temptation and has patiently endured testing and trials. There are people who suffer from physical infirmities or bad marriages or poverty or emotional trials that are no fault of their own. Others, at this very moment, are suffering for their testimony of Jesus Christ in different parts of the world.

God says, "I have a special crown for you who have endured difficult situations and consistently resisted temptation."

There will be a crown of righteousness.

Shortly before his execution in a Roman dungeon, the apostle Paul wrote these words to his young friend, Timothy:

> The time of my departure is at hand. I have fought the good fight, I have finished the race, I have kept the faith. Finally, there is laid up for me the crown of righteousness, which the Lord, the righteous Judge, will give to me on that Day, and not to me only but also to all who have loved His appearing. (2 Timothy 4:6-8)

This is a crown that will be given specifically to those who have served God and have a heart for heaven.

Do you long for the return of Jesus Christ? Then there is a crown waiting for you. There is also a crown waiting for you if you have remained faithful to the Lord, and finished the race He set out before you.

So make every day of your life count, my friend. Keep one foot in heaven and keep another foot on earth, and be ready to meet your God.

He's coming soon.

And those aren't my words, they are His.

Conclusion
THE JONAH SIGN

A s we wrap up this book together, let's circle the airplane back to the passage where Jesus first coined the phrase "signs of the times."

Some Pharisees and Sadducees were on him again, pressing him to prove himself to them. He told them, "You have a saying that goes, 'Red sky at night, sailor's delight; red sky at morning, sailors take warning.' You find it easy enough to forecast the weather—why can't you read the signs of the times? An evil and wanton generation is always wanting signs and wonders. The only sign you'll get is the Jonah sign." Then he turned on his heel and walked away. (Matthew 16:1-4, THE MESSAGE)

In essence, Jesus says to these faithless, cynical religious leaders, "I won't show you any more signs. You've seen more than enough. But there will be one last sign I will give you, and you can take it or leave it. It will be the sign of the prophet Jonah."

He knew they had no intention of believing in the first place

He also knew they would close their eyes to His last and greatest sign: dying for the sins of the world, being buried in the earth for three days, and then rising again. Just as Jonah was swallowed up by the great fish, and resurfaced three days later, so Jesus would be swallowed by death. But death would never be able hold Him. After three days, He would come out of that tomb, alive forever.

The Pharisees and Sadducees asked Him for a big dramatic sign in the sky. But even that wouldn't have made any difference. He could have written across the sky in letters half a mile high, "Jesus is Lord," but they would have only ignored it or explained it away. They had so hardened their hearts that they simply *refused* to believe.

In the Lord's parable in Luke 16, a rich man in hell cried out to Abraham, in Paradise, to send Lazarus the beggar from the dead to persuade his unbelieving brothers to turn to God. But Abraham replied, "If they do not hear Moses and the prophets, neither will they be persuaded though one rise from the dead" (v. 31).

In other words, signs and wonders just won't cut it when it comes to someone turning to Jesus Christ. It has to be an act of the will. It has to be a decision of the heart.

The fact is, ten million signs and wonders in the church today would not make the world turn to Christ. On a smaller scale, maybe you've thought to yourself, *If I could just do some kind of miracle in front of my friends, they would be so blown away they'd become Christians.*

No, they probably wouldn't.

When a person genuinely places his or her faith in Jesus Christ as Savior and Lord, it is because he or she has taken a step of faith and made the decision to reach out toward God. And what they will always find is that He is already reaching out to them.

Jesus told them, "You want a sign? Here's My sign. I will die on a cross for the sins of the world. I will be placed in a tomb. And I will rise from the dead three days later."

Contrary to what we might hope or believe, some dramatic miracle will never convince someone to surrender to Jesus Christ. Think about it. Jesus raised Lazarus from the dead, and everyone knew it. And what happened immediately after that? They began plotting to kill Jesus *and* Lazarus, to remove the evidence. (See John 12:9-11)

Poor Lazarus. Wasn't it bad enough that he had to die once? And then they wanted to *kill* him? Why? Because Lazarus was a living, breathing miracle. His very presence gave testimony to the power of God.

And guess what? You too are a living, breathing miracle-man or miracle-woman if you tell others about how God has changed your life, and transformed you. You are a powerful representative of Jesus Christ.

So get up in the morning with the determination that, God helping you, you will *be* that representative.

So what is our message to a lost world?

"Hey, everybody gather round…. We're going to have a miracle service here, do a bunch of miracles, and then everyone will believe. We'll walk down the line touching people, and they will collapse on the floor, and that will impress the world."

No, that's not going to do it.

Here is how Paul summarized his message and his methodology in 1 Corinthians 2:

> Dear brothers and sisters, when I first came to you I didn't use lofty words and brilliant ideas to tell you God's message. For I decided to concentrate only on Jesus Christ and his death on the cross. I came to you in weakness—timid and trembling. And my message and my preaching were very plain. I did not use wise and persuasive speeches, but the Holy Spirit was powerful among you. I did this so that you might trust the power of God rather than human wisdom. (vv. 1-5, NLT)

Paul's "method" was to simply proclaim the gospel. And what is the gospel? That we are all sinners, and separated from God. But God so loved the world that He sent His one and only Son to die on the cross, paying the penalty for our sins, and then raising Him from the dead. *That* is the gospel. Don't apologize for it, don't add to it, and don't gloss it over. Just proclaim it and watch what God will do.

Recently I received a letter from an outlaw biker. Here is what he wrote.

> Hello Pastor Greg.

> I have to share this with you. New Year's Eve of 1999 I listened to a radio program of years, and was amazed at your teaching and the way you presented the gospel message. I had heard the message all my life and I just didn't believe it. It seemed like a fairy tale to me.

> During this time I was an outlaw biker and I was sick of the life I was living. I had no joy or hope in it and I decided I was going to kill myself the night that I heard you. But I went to turn on my stereo to

listen to some music while I went out. I couldn't get a station to come on except the local Christian radio station. And your voice came on and I listened and I heard what you said about Jesus Christ and His offer of forgiveness.

I cried out to God. I prayed, "God if You are real, make yourself real to me, or I'm going to just stick this needle in my arm and find out for myself." Well, God rained down His Spirit on me, and I was awash in this unbelievable love and joy and sense of forgiveness. The sense of heaviness I had carried on my back was physically lifted off of me, and I started to cry like a baby.

Last June, I graduated from Bible college with a BA in theology. I've become an ordained minister, working with children, and a chaplain with the Christian Motorcyclists Association where I go out and minister to other outlaw bikers.

That is the power of the gospel. And that is our message to this culture, and to our world. *Jesus Christ crucified, and risen again from the dead.*

That is the "sign of Jonah," and it's still the greatest sign of all.

A Heartbeat from Eternity

Jesus Christ is coming back again! The signs all around us remind us of that fact. And that means we could be hurtled into eternity in the blink of an eye.

I saw a trailer the other night for a movie called "Source Code." Apparently, it's the story of a man who has the ability to cross over into another man's identity in the last eight minutes of his life. At one point he asks a woman, "What would you do if these were the last minutes of your life?" And she answers, "I would make those minutes count."

That's just what you and I need to be doing right now. None of us knows how much time we have left on earth—whether it's 8 minutes, 8 days, 8 months, 8 years or 80 years.

But we do know this much. Eternity can be upon us in an instant. It can happen through the Lord's coming, or it can happen at death.

That is why you need to be prepared and ready to meet the Lord at all times, because you don't know when the end will come. It may not be the end of THE world, but it could be the end of YOUR world.

Time once spent, can't be recycled. It's like a coin; once you spend it, you can't spend it again. It's gone.

When I was little boy, I remember that someone gave me a dollar and said, "Greg, if you will hold on to this dollar all day long, and save it at the end of the day, I will give you five more dollars."

Well, that sounded like a pretty good deal. So I held onto that dollar all morning, and almost all afternoon. Almost. The deal was, I was supposed to hang onto it until 5:00. At around 4:15, however, I couldn't contain myself. I went down to the little drugstore near our home and spent the dollar. I even remember what I bought. It was a little skull head on a leather band. When you held it under a lamp and then shut the lights off, it glowed in the dark. I also remember that it smelled like rotting eggs.

The man who had made the offer to me came at 5:00, and I had to tell him what I'd done. He just shook his head. "Greg," he said, if you had waited thirty more minutes, I would have give you five more bucks. You could have had your little skull and more money besides."

"I know," I said, hanging my head. I felt stupid because I had squandered my money—and my opportunity.

In a much, much larger sense, God has given you years of life—an infinitely precious commodity. Each and every day, we get so many hours and minutes deposited to our account, to use or neglect.

But then the day will come (whether we're aware of it or not) when we are down to our last minute. We need to use that time well.

Paul wrote,

> Live life, then, with a due sense of responsibility, not as men who do not know the meaning and purpose of life but as those who do. Make the best use of your time, despite all the difficulties of these days. Don't be vague but firmly grasp what you know to be the will of God. (Ephesians 5:15-17, PHILLIPS)

In Romans 13, he adds these words:

> As I think you have realised, the present time is of the highest importance —it is time to wake up to reality. Every day brings God's salvation nearer. The night is nearly over, the day has almost dawned. Let us therefore fling away the things that men do in the dark, let us arm ourselves for the fight of the day! Let us live cleanly, as in the daylight, not in the "delights" of getting drunk or playing with sex, nor yet in quarrelling or jealousies. Let us be Christ's men from head to foot, and give no chances to the flesh to have its fling. (vv. 11-14, PHILLIPS)

The day is close. Be ready to meet your God.

ENDNOTES

1   From an Interview on CBS, (October 5, 1956). Accessed at: http://en.wikiquote. org/wiki/David_Ben-Gurion

2   Taheri, Amir. "Whose vision will build the new Egypt?" *New York Post* (March 5, 2011). Accessed at: http://www.nypost.com/p/news/opinion/opedcolumnists/ whose_vision_will_build_the_new_0BKAOIk7OubFWeKDdl4HaJ

3   Mahmoud Ahmadinejad, "The World Without Zionism," Tehran (October 26, 2005). Quoted from the MEMRI translation (October 28, 2005). Accessed at: http://www.memri.org/report/en/0/0/0/0/0/0/0/1510.htm.

4   Tim LaHaye, *The Rapture* (Eugene, OR: Harvest House Publishers, 2002), 88.

5   Hal Lindsey, *Apocalypse Code* (Palos Verdes, CA: Western Front Ltd., 1997), 296.

6   See Matthew 24:8

7   See 1 Corinthians 15:52

8   See Matthew 6

9   http://en.wikipedia.org/wiki/History_of_Israel#The_State_of_Israel_declared

10 Charles Haddon Spurgeon, *The Metropolitan Tabernacle pulpit:* sermons, Parts 453-464 (General Books, 2009), 164

11 See 1 Timothy 4:1

12 Jeffrey L. Sheerer and Mike Tharp, "Dark Prophesies," *U.S. News and World Report* (December 15, 1997).

13 Steven Levy "Playing the ID Card," *Newsweek* (May 13, 2002).

14 http://en.wikipedia.org/wiki/Doomsday Clock

15 See Matthew 24:4-5

16 Malcolm Muggeridge in verbal communication

17 Erwin Lutzer, *Hitler's Cross* (Chicago, IL: Moody Press, 1995), 16.

18 Joel C. Rosenberg, "Today in Bible Prophecy" Blog, http://www.todayinbibleprophecy.org/n/world_leaders_consider_single_global_currency.html

19 Hal Lindsey, *The Late Great Planet Earth* (Grand Rapids, MI: Zondervan, 1970), 130.

20 Paul-Henri Spaak, "Council of Europe," 1949.

21 From T.S. Eliot's poem "The Hollow Men."

22 See Luke 21:29-33

23 John Walvoord, in Tim LaHaye, Jerry Jenkins, *Are We Living In The End Times?* (Wheaton, IL: Tyndale House Publishers, Inc., 1999), 47.

24 Benjamin Netanyahu at ceremony marking 65 years since the liberation of the Auschwitz (January 27, 2010). Accessed at: http://www.worldjewishcongress. org/en/main/showNews/id/8854?print=true

25 Alexei Borodavkin, "Russia set to boost military-technical ties with Iran," http:// www.presstv.ir/detail.aspx?id=108016&sectionid=351020101

26 Mahmoud Ahmadinejad, speech to UN United Nations, New York (September 17, 2005). Text in http://www.globalsecurity.org/wmd/library/news/iran/2005/ iran-050918-irna02.htm

27 Cleric Mojtaba Zolnour, State IRNA news agency. Quoted in an AP story in the *Tehran Times* (www.tehrantimes.com/politics)

28 General Effie Eitam, in a wide-ranging briefing for journalists, hosted by *One Jerusalem* (January 7, 2009).

29 C. S. Lewis, *Mere Christianity: A Revised And Amplified Edition* (New York, NY: HarperCollins, 1980), 116.

30 Gallup Poll, http://www.gallup.com

31 Jeremiah, David. *What in the World is Going On* (Nashville, TN: Thomas Nelson, 2008), 189.

32 Douglas Brinkley, ed., *The Reagan Diaries* (New York, NY: HarperCollins, 2007), 19.

33 *Ibid*, 24.

34 Jeremiah, David. *What in the World is Going On*, 194.

35 Fareed Zakaria, *Newsweek*, May 9, 2005, http://www.fareedzakaria.com/articles/newsweek/050905.html

36 *Ibid*.

37 Accessed at: http://blog.dailyalert.org/2011/02/03/wikileaks-al-qaeda-on-the-verge-of-producing-radioactive-weapons/

38 See 2 Timothy 3:5

39 See Exodus 12:14-20

40 The incident is documented in Ralston's autobiography, *Between a Rock and a Hard Place*, and is the subject of the 2010 film, *127 Hours*.

41 "Tiger Woods and Buddhism" (February 19, 2010). Accessed at: http://www.cbsnews.com/stories/2010/02/19/sportsline/main6223844.shtml

42 Cannon, Carl M. "Fox, Tiger, and Christianity" Accessed at: http://www.politics-daily.com/2010/01/08/fox-tiger-and-christianity-a-defense-of-brit-hume/

43 MacArthur, John. *Think Biblically* (Wheaton, IL: Crossway, 2003), 14.

44 Mark Twain quote accessed at: http://www.twainquotes.com/Father.html

45 *The Lucado Life Lessons Study Bible* (Nashville, TN: Thomas Nelson, 2010), 64.

46 Nancy Gibbs; Sam Allis/Boston, Nancy Harbert/Angel Fire and Lisa H. Towle/Raleigh, with other bureaus "Angels Among Us". *Time* (December 27, 1993). Accessed at: http://www.time.com/time/magazine/article/0,9171,979893-9,00.html#ixzz0gavW9pJj

47 Graham, Billy. *Angels: God's Secret Agents* (Nashville, TN: Thomas Nelson, 2007), 5.

48 C. S. Lewis, *The Screwtape Letters* (New York, NY: HarperCollins, 2001), ix.

49 See Revelation 12:4

50 See 1 Peter 5:8

51 See John 10:10

52 See 2 Corinthians 11:14

53 See 2 Corinthians 10:5

54 See Matthew 26:47-50

55 See Matthew 27:5

56 See Matthew 26:74-75

57 Woody Allen, cited in Greg Laurie, *Why Believe?* (Wheaton, IL: Tyndale House Publishers, Inc., 2002), 76.

58 Jim Carrey quote accessed at: http://einstein/quotes/jim_carrey

59 J. I. Packer. Original source unknown, accessed at: http://johnsnotes.com/archives/end_times/03_05_04_Hell2.shtml

60 See 1 Corinthians 5:6-8

61 Rosemarie Jarski, *Words from the Wise: Over 6,000 of the Smartest Things Ever Said* (New York, NY: Skyhorse Publishing, Inc., 2007), 162.

62 See 1 Corinthians 15:6

63 Robert De Niro. From an interview on *Inside the Actors Studio* (31 January 1999).

64 See Matthew 25:41

65 J. I. Packer, *Concise Theology: A Guide to Historic Christian Beliefs* (Wheaton, IL: Tyndale House Publishers, Inc., 2001), 263-264.

66 C. S. Lewis, *The Great Divorce* (New York, NY: Macmillan, 1963), 69.

67 Timothy Keller, "The Importance of Hell". Accessed at http://www.redeemer.com/news_and_events/articles/the_importance_of_hell.html.

68 Pat Williams and Jim Denney, *How to Be Like Walt: Capturing the Disney Magic Every Day of Your Life* (Deerfield Beach, FL: HCI, 2004), 325.

69 See Ecclesiastes 3:11

70 St. Augustine (Bishop of Hippo), *The Confessions*, I:1.

71 C. S. Lewis, *The Problem of Pain* (Clearwater, FL: Touchstone Books, 1996), 30.

72 Edward McKendree Bounds, *Heaven: A Place, a City, a Home* (Grand Rapids, MI: Revell Co., 1921).

73 Warren Wiersbe, *The Wiersbe Bible Commentary: The Complete New Testament* (David C. Cook, 2007), 516.

74 Randy Alcorn, *Heaven*.

75 See Exodus 33:18-23

76 Rosemarie Jarski, *Words from the Wise: Over 6,000 of the Smartest Things Ever Said* (Skyhorsepublishing, 2007), 18.

77 Randy Alcorn, *Heaven*, 265.

78 See 2 Corinthians 12:4

79 C. S. Lewis and Clyde Kilby, *A Mind Awake: An Anthology of C. S. Lewis* (Houghton-Mifflin, 1968), 184.

80 C. S. Lewis, *Mere Christianity*, 134.

81 See Ecclesiastes 3:11

82 C. S. Lewis, *Mere Christianity*, 137.

83 Joni Eareckson Tada, *Heaven: Your Real Home* (Grand Rapids, MI: Zondervan, 1995), 34.

84 Graham, Billy. *Just As I Am* (New York, NY: HarperCollins, 1998), 848.

85 D. L. Moody, cited in Greg Laurie, *Why Believe?*, 77.

86 Randy Alcorn, *Heaven*, 336.

87 C. S. Lewis, *Mere Christianity*, 116.

88 See 1 Corinthians 3:6-8

89 John Charles Pollock, *Billy Graham, Evangelist to the World: an Authorized Biography of the Decisive Years* (New York, NY: Harper & Row, 1979),113.

ALLEN DAVID BOOKS Other AllenDavid Books Published by Kerygma Publishing

Visit: www.kerygmapublishing.com
www.allendavidbooks.com

KERYGMA PUBLISHING